S. Hrg. 113–575

REAUTHORIZATION OF THE SATELLITE TELEVISION EXTENSION AND LOCALISM ACT

HEARING

BEFORE THE

SUBCOMMITTEE ON COMMUNICATIONS, TECHNOLOGY, AND THE INTERNET

OF THE

COMMITTEE ON COMMERCE, SCIENCE, AND TRANSPORTATION UNITED STATES SENATE

ONE HUNDRED THIRTEENTH CONGRESS

SECOND SESSION

———

APRIL 1, 2014

———

Printed for the use of the Committee on Commerce, Science, and Transportation

U.S. GOVERNMENT PUBLISHING OFFICE

93–480 PDF   WASHINGTON : 2015

(II)

CONTENTS

REAUTHORIZATION OF THE SATELLITE TELEVISION EXTENSION AND LOCALISM ACT

TUESDAY, APRIL 1, 2014

U.S. SENATE,
SUBCOMMITTEE ON COMMUNICATIONS, TECHNOLOGY, AND
THE INTERNET,
COMMITTEE ON COMMERCE, SCIENCE, AND TRANSPORTATION,
Washington, DC.

The Subcommittee met, pursuant to notice, at 3:05 p.m. in room SR–253, Russell Senate Office Building, Hon. Mark Pryor, Chairman of the Subcommittee, presiding.

OPENING STATEMENT OF HON. MARK PRYOR,
U.S. SENATOR FROM ARKANSAS

Senator PRYOR. I'll go ahead and call our meeting to order.

Thank you all for being here. And, I'm sorry we had to postpone for about 35 minutes based on the originally scheduled time because of the votes on the floor. And also, I know that Chairman Rockefeller is on his way and many others are on their way as well.

So again, I want to thank you all for being here. This is the reauthorization of the Satellite Television Extension and Localism Act hearing. And I know that many of you had to change schedules to be here and did a lot of preparation to be here.

So STELA, and its legislative predecessors, have served to help satellite television operators provide their subscribers with access to broadcast TV channels thus allowing these companies to compete on a level playing field with other providers in the video marketplace. The driving force behind these laws are the worthy goals of ensuring not only that consumers have access to the programming they desire, but that they have a choice of provider in a competitive marketplace that fosters better content, more services, and lower prices.

And let's not forget that these laws have helped DISH Network and DIRECTV offer to many millions of customers over the years, primarily rural customers, at least in my state, the ability to purchase pay-TV services in areas not previously served by other pay-TV providers.

Once again, with provisions within STELA set to expire at the end of the year, we have the opportunity to revisit and reconsider these policies. Our colleagues in the House and Senate Judiciary Committee have begun their efforts in earnest. And I'm glad all of you could be here today to discuss the Commerce Committee's pieces, I'll say pieces, plural, of this law.

Well, I know that there are some who believe that STELA's time has passed and it should not be renewed. We cannot lose sight of the approximately 1.5 million people who may be harmed by STELA's expiration. As a result, I believe that the Congress should act to reauthorize STELA before it expires at the end of the year. With that said, I want you all to know that I'm approaching our reauthorization efforts with an open mind and that is why I've joined Senator Rockefeller, Thune, and Wicker in seeking comment for a diverse group of stakeholders on the appropriate scope of the reauthorization.

We have a large panel today containing some familiar faces with the Subcommittee's "State of Video" hearing just last year. It's particularly nice to have our former colleague, Senator Smith, back with us.

So welcome back to the Subcommittee. It's always great to see you.

I hope to hear from our witnesses about the provisions of STELA that are expiring and how they have or have not been working for consumers. And I know they have been honing their arguments before other committees. So we appreciate you being here.

I also know that many of you will want to talk about a host of other issues that some stakeholders would like to see potentially addressed as part of this reauthorization. I certainly look forward to hearing from all of you, but I want to reiterate my view that what ultimately matters in this debate and, more importantly, in legislation that would be considered by this committee, is what is best for the consumer.

Folks back home are less interested in what goes on behind the scenes than making sure that they can receive broadcast TV programming relevant to their lives; whether it be news important to their communities, their favorite sports teams, or, more critically, timely weather warnings that can ultimately save lives.

So, I look forward to working with all of you. And I look forward to working with my colleagues, as well, on the STELA reauthorization.

Again, I want to say thank you for being here. And, with that, I'll recognize Senator Wicker.

STATEMENT OF HON. ROGER F. WICKER,
U.S. SENATOR FROM MISSISSIPPI

Senator WICKER. Thank you, Chairman Pryor, for holding this hearing on reauthorization of the Satellite Television Extension and Localism Act, better known as "STELA."

This hearing is timely considering recent action at both ends of the Capitol. Last week, the House Subcommittee on Communications marked up and reported its version of STELA. And the Senate Judiciary Committee, which shares jurisdiction with this committee, held its own hearing on the topic. The expiration of the current STELA has brought discussion regarding not only issues surrounding the satellite industry. On a broader scale, it has led the debate on the current state of the video marketplace in the digital broadband era. This debate has proven quite instructive with plenty of divergent opinions offered.

Many of those policy positions came in the form of detailed and informed answers to the letters Senator Pryor and I sent with Chairman Rockefeller and Ranking Member Thune. The letters sent to stakeholders, across the industry, directly solicited feedback on the key issues surrounding the STELA debate and provided a good sound foundation for this committee to build on as it moves forward.

All of the private sector witnesses on this panel received a letter and all answered the questions in a thoughtful and complete fashion. Thank you for doing that. The entire Subcommittee thanks you for your input and looks forward to hearing you expand on your positions as we examine these issues further.

Mr. Chairman, sending this letter together kick-started this process in a bipartisan way and it is my hope that we will continue on that path.

The House was able to achieve a working consensus on a set of narrow, targeted, common sense reforms many of which are sure to be discussed this afternoon. Given the history of this committee, I'm confident that we will be able to work in a similar fashion.

So, thank you to our witnesses for testifying today. Your presence here will give members an opportunity to gain your take on issues specific to STELA as well as many issues the FCC is considering in the interconnected media landscape.

So thank you very much for being here. And thank you, Mr. Chairman.

Senator PRYOR. Thank you, Senator Wicker.

What we're going to do right now is I'll go ahead and recognize the panel. I'll just introduce you as a group and we'll go one-by-one. But also, when Senator Rockefeller shows up, I know he can only be here a short time. I'll probably, you know, let you finish the statement that we're on at the moment and then let the Chairman make his opening statement.

And that may also be the same as Senator Thune. I think he was going to stay longer but now that we pushed this back I don't know exactly what his schedule is, but I don't want to be disruptive but, certainly, we want them to have an opportunity to make their opening statement.

So I'll just run down the table here real quickly and introduce everyone and then we'll call on Mr. Lake to lead us off.

Mr. William T. Lake, Chief, Media Bureau, Federal Communications Commission; the Honorable Gordon Smith, President and Chief Executive Officer of the National Association of Broadcasters, again, we welcome you back to the Subcommittee; Mr. Michael W. Palkovic, Executive Vice President, Operations, DIRECTV; the Honorable Michael K. Powell, President and Chief Executive Officer of the National Cable and Telecommunications Association, always good to see you; Mr. Thomas S. Rogers, President and Chief Executive Officer of TiVo; and also, Mr. Matt Wood, Policy Director of Free Press.

So again, thank you all for joining us.

Mr. Lake.

STATEMENT OF WILLIAM T. LAKE, CHIEF, MEDIA BUREAU, FEDERAL COMMUNITICATIONS COMMISSION

Mr. LAKE. Thank you.

Good afternoon, Chairman Pryor, Ranking Member Wicker and members of the Subcommittee. My name is Bill Lake, and I'm the Chief of the Media Bureau at the Federal Communications Commission. I'm grateful for the opportunity to appear before you today as the Subcommittee begins to evaluate reauthorization of STELA.

As the Subcommittee knows, but a quick reminder is always helpful, unless reauthorized by Congress, there are two provisions in the Communications Act that will expire at the end of this year: the authorization for satellite operators to retransmit distant network signals to an unserved household without first obtaining the consent of the station; and the sections that prohibit broadcast stations from engaging in exclusive contracts for carriage, and require both broadcasters and pay-TV operators, MVPDs, to negotiate in good faith for retransmission consent.

In addition, it's important to note that the distant signal copyright license will also expire, which will affect current and grandfathered subscribers, as well as future subscribers who meet STELA's eligibility requirements to receive distant signals. I provide as an attachment to my statement a broad historical background on congressional action in this area, beginning with the enactment of the Satellite Home Viewer Act, over 25 years ago, and continuing through the most recent reauthorization, STELA.

Also included is information on how the concurrent rules work for consumers today. I hope that this will help to inform the Subcommittee about the evolution of the provisions under consideration. I note that there are other issues that have been brought up in the context of this reauthorization process by both the Committee and stakeholder representatives, some of whom are with me here today. But I will limit these remarks to the specific topic at hand.

Historically, Commission staff has provided Congress with technical assistance as it works through issues related to the expiring provisions, and we continue to stand-at-the-ready as you and other congressional committees continue to work on the reauthorization.

Additionally, as always, the Commission will be tasked with implementing any changes that Congress makes to the language in the Communications Act. Having noted that, if we have one ask for Congress at this juncture, from the staff who worked directly on these issues, it would be for Congress to keep in mind the interdependence of the Communications Act provisions with the Copyright Act statutory licenses. While I understand that the Commerce and Judiciary Committees on both sides work very well to develop the underlying policies, ensuring that the statutory language is complementary between the two acts is essential to make sure that the intent of Congress is effectuated.

Again, thank you for the opportunity to be here today. And I'll be happy to take any questions you have.

[The prepared statement of Mr. Lake follows:]

PREPARED STATEMENT OF WILLIAM T. LAKE, CHIEF, MEDIA BUREAU,
FEDERAL COMMUNICATIONS COMMISSION

Good afternoon, Chairman Pryor, Ranking Member Wicker, and Members of the Subcommittee. My name is Bill Lake, and I am the Chief of the Media Bureau at the Federal Communications Commission. I'm grateful for the opportunity to appear before you today as the Subcommittee begins to evaluate reauthorization of the Satellite Television Extension and Localism Act of 2010—commonly known as STELA.

As the Subcommittee knows—but a quick reminder is always helpful—unless reauthorized by Congress, there are two provisions in the Communications Act that will expire at the end of this year:

- The authorization for satellite operators to *retransmit distant network signals* to an unserved household without first obtaining the consent of the station; and

- The sections prohibiting broadcast stations from engaging in *exclusive contracts* for carriage, and requiring both broadcasters and MVPDs to *negotiate in good faith* for retransmission consent.

In addition, it is important to note that the distant signal copyright license will also expire, which will affect current and grandfathered subscribers as well as future subscribers who meet STELA's eligibility requirements to receive distant signals.

I provide as an attachment to my statement a broad historical background on Congressional action in this area, beginning with the enactment of the Satellite Home Viewer Act over 25 years ago and continuing through the most recent reauthorization, STELA. Also included is information on how the current rules work for consumers today. I hope that this will help to inform the Subcommittee about the evolution of the provisions under consideration.

I note that there are other issues that have been brought up in the context of this reauthorization process—by both the Committee and stakeholder representatives (some of whom are with me here today). But I will limit these remarks to the specific topic at hand.

Historically, Commission staff has provided Congress with technical assistance as it works through issues related to the expiring provisions, and we continue to stand at the ready as you and the other Congressional Committees continue to work on the reauthorization. Additionally, as always, the Commission will be tasked with implementing any changes that Congress makes to the language in the Communications Act.

Having noted that, if we have one ask for Congress at this juncture—from the staff who work directly on these issues—it would be for Congress to keep in mind the interdependence of the Communications Act provisions with the Copyright Act statutory licenses. While I understand that the Commerce and Judiciary Committees on both sides work together very well to develop the underlying policies, ensuring that the statutory language is complementary between the two Acts is essential to make sure that the intent of Congress is effectuated.

Again, thank you for the opportunity to be here today. I'll be happy to take any questions you may have.

————

ATTACHMENT

History of Satellite TV Law

SHVA

It has been over 25 years since Congress first established a statutory copyright license to give satellite carriers the ability to provide consumers with broadcast programming via satellite. The Satellite Home Viewer Act of 1988 (SHVA) and subsequent reauthorizations amend provisions in the Communications Act and in the copyright statute, Title 17.

At the time of SHVA, satellite carriers were technologically limited in the number of broadcast channels they could deliver to their subscribers. SHVA was intended to provide a means for those carriers to offer the broadcast network programming while protecting the role of local broadcasters. SHVA thus limited satellite delivery of network broadcast programming to subscribers who were "unserved" by over-the-air signals. It also permitted carriers to offer distant "superstations" to subscribers. "Unserved" was defined as a household that did not receive an over-the-air signal of a particular signal strength from any station affiliated with a particular network. SHVA endorsed the Commission's computer model that predicts signal strength at a specific location, now known as the Individual Location Longley-Rice (or ILLR) predictive model. The predictive model was coupled with a process by which a subscriber who was predicted to be served could request a waiver from the relevant local stations, and, if the waiver was denied, could request an actual signal test.

SHVIA

The Satellite Home Viewer Improvement Act of 1999 (SHVIA) expanded opportunities for consumers by creating a framework for satellite carriers to retransmit *local* broadcast signals directly to subscribers through a new local signal copyright license—commonly known as "local-into-local" service. Beginning with SHVIA and continuing today, "local stations" are determined based on the Nielsen Designated Market Areas (DMAs) and typically by reference to the DMA map. In contrast to the "must carry" requirements that apply nationwide to cable service, the law requires satellite operators to carry all qualified local stations on a market-by-market basis (using DMAs) only if the satellite carrier opts to carry any local station in the market by reliance on the statutory copyright license. This is known as the "carry one, carry all" requirement.[1] The Commission implemented SHVIA by adopting rules for satellite carriers with regard to carriage of broadcast signals, retransmission consent, and program exclusivity. These rules are comparable to the requirements for cable service.

In addition to introducing the legislative and regulatory mechanism by which satellite carriers can offer "local" stations to subscribers, SHVIA also maintained the mechanism for unserved subscribers to receive distant network stations, with a few tweaks to the waiver and testing protocol and still with reliance on the Commission's predictive model in the first instance.

SHVERA

In 2004, Congress continued to expand and develop parity between satellite and cable services when it enacted the Satellite Home Viewer Extension and Reauthorization Act (SHVERA) and provided the framework for satellite carriage of "significantly viewed" stations. Significantly viewed stations are those that technically are distant signals—*i.e.,* assigned to another DMA—but historically had "significant" over-the-air viewing in specific communities or counties in a neighboring DMA. The Commission has maintained a "significantly viewed" list since the 1970s. In addition, if a station meets the significantly viewed criteria for a particular community or county, it can petition the Commission to be added to this list. Carriage of such stations is voluntary on the part of the satellite carriers and requires the retransmission consent of the significantly viewed station. Only subscribers in the specific community or county who subscribe to the local-into-local service are eligible to receive the significantly viewed station from out of market. SHVERA also imposed additional restrictions on the carriage of digital significantly viewed stations—requiring that the local station affiliated with the same network is provided in the same format.[2]

In addition to the significantly viewed provisions, Congress also modified the statutory language to account for various digital television transition issues, imposed the good-faith bargaining requirements for retransmission consent negotiations on multichannel video program distributors, and provided for some exceptions to the distant copyright license for certain areas of the country.

STELA

The Satellite Television Extension and Localism Act (STELA), enacted in 2010, is the most recent iteration in the series of statutes that address satellite carriage of television broadcast stations. In addition to reauthorizing the expiring provisions of law, the major provisions of STELA include changes to the significantly viewed provisions enacted in SHVERA to promote use of the statutory provisions and provide additional choices for subscribers.[3] Congress also modified the law to account for the terrestrial digital television transition that occurred in 2009 by requiring the Commission to establish a digital signal predictive model and to revise its measurement procedures for determining eligibility for subscribers to receive distant digital

---

[1] Satellite carriers are allowed to exclude from their local-into-local service stations that are duplicative or stations that fail to provide a good quality signal to the satellite carrier's local receive facility. Satellite subscribers are not generally required to subscribe to the local-into-local package.

[2] There were two exceptions to these restrictions on the carriage of significantly viewed stations—(1) satellite carriers could provide a significantly viewed station in areas where there was no local affiliate station; and (2) satellite carriers could negotiate a waiver with the local affiliate with regards to carriage of a significantly viewed station. Note that STELA's revisions affect these exceptions. *See infra* n. 5 and associated text, and n. 9.

[3] Congress also moved the corresponding copyright provisions for significantly viewed stations from the distant signal copyright license to the local signal copyright license.

signals.[4] Congress also changed the definition of the stations considered when determining whether a subscriber is served or unserved by an over-the-air signal for the purpose of eligibility for satellite-delivered distant signals; specified how multicast signals would be treated; and introduced the concept of "short" markets, that is, DMAs with fewer than four of the most widely viewed networks.[5] Additionally, Congress required the Commission to provide a report to Congress regarding the availability of in-state programming for those counties that are assigned to a DMA served primarily by stations that are licensed to a different state.

Practical Application of Current Law and Rules

Local-into-Local Service

Since the inception of local-into-local service, the two satellite providers have increased their local market offerings to the point where subscribers in most, if not all, of the 210 local markets (DMAs) have access to the local package by one or both of the providers. The specifics are outlined below:

Date/Timing	DISH	DirecTV	Source
Nov. 2000	34	38	FCC 7th Video Competition Report
Dec. 2004	150 (+PR)	130	FCC 11th Video Competition Report
Fall 2007	174	143	FCC 13th Video Competition Report
Fall 2012	210	194	SEC Filings
February 2013	210	196	STELA Section 305 Report
Nov. 2013	210	197*	STELA Section 305 Report

*Markets currently without Local-into-Local service from DirecTV: Presque Isle ME; Alpena MI; Charlottesville VA; Victoria TX; Ottumwa IA-Kirksville MO; San Angelo TX; Bowling Green KY; North Platte NE; Cheyenne WY-Scottsbluff NE; Helena MT; Casper-Riverton WY; Grand Junction-Montrose CO; Glendive MT.

A consumer can subscribe to satellite service from one of the two providers, and opt for different program packages. As part of the available packages, consumers can opt to subscribe to the local channel package for an additional charge. The local channels will be those stations that are assigned to the DMA in which the consumer resides based on the Nielsen designations. Consumers are not allowed to choose the local stations they wish to receive via satellite, and satellite providers are limited in the stations they are permitted to include in the local package. As noted above, Congress has allowed for additional flexibility in certain circumstances that could increase the choices available to subscribers, such as permitting carriage of significantly viewed stations in appropriate circumstances.

As noted above, if a carrier chooses to provide any significantly viewed stations from the FCC's list, it can add those stations to the local package offerings after obtaining the retransmission consent of the station. Additionally, there are certain areas in the country in which Congress provided an exception to the copyright license to allow carriage into specific counties of additional signals that would otherwise be considered distant signals.

Distant Signals

Distant signals, generally, are those broadcast stations that are assigned to a different DMA than the one in which the consumer resides. In the past, distant signals provided the only access to broadcast network programming for many satellite subscribers. Over time, more and more subscribers gained access to the local network stations via local-into-local service. Even so, much of STELA, like its predecessors, is devoted to the requirements and limitations associated with eligibility for distant signals. The following is an overview of the highlights and concepts.

Generally, in order to be eligible to receive distant signals, a subscriber must be deemed to be "unserved" by the local signals via an over-the-air antenna. "Unserved" means that the subscriber's household cannot receive the over-the-air signal of a local network station with sufficient signal strength[6] as outlined in the

---

[4] Congress revised the definition of "unserved household" to eliminate a specific reference to "outdoor" antennas. The Commission rulemaking determined that, from an engineering and technical perspective, consideration of an outdoor measurement remains preferable.

[5] Prior to STELA, the signal of any station affiliated with a particular network was considered in determining whether a subscriber was "served" or "unserved" by that network. STELA established that only network stations that are in the subscriber's "local" market (i.e., the same DMA) would be considered in making this determination. This change facilitated providing missing network stations via satellite to subscribers in short markets.

[6] STELA more specifically defines sufficient strength as the intensity defined by the FCC as the value for the "noise-limited service contour," which means the value associated with a station's coverage area.

current rules.[7] Additionally, subscribers are limited to no more than 2 network-affiliated signals from each broadcast network. If a subscriber is also receiving local stations, STELA restricts the time shifting permissible for the distant signals based on the subscriber's local time zone. Generally, the subscriber cannot specify which distant signals he or she wishes to receive. In addition to the eligibility criteria associated with the subscriber, the satellite carrier is permitted to provide distant signals only if it complies with the requirement to provide the networks with lists of the subscribers who are receiving distant signals. Below are some of the other major provisions regarding distant signals.

No Distant Where Local

When new consumers subscribe to satellite TV service, and the local-into-local package is available via satellite, they are not eligible to receive distant signals under current law. We refer to this as "no distant where local."

One exception to no-distant-where-local is if the local signals are provided in the DMA but the subscriber lives in an area that is technically outside of the spot beam used to provide the local signals. In those instances, the subscriber will be permitted to receive the distant signals if the subscriber is also "unserved" by local stations over-the-air.

No Local-into-Local Service

If the consumer resides in a market where their preferred satellite carrier does not offer a local-into-local package, they may be able to receive a distant signal package if they are "unserved." The subscriber requests distant signals through his or her satellite carrier, and the carrier determines whether there is a sufficient signal by using a computer model that predicts the signal strength at the subscriber's specific household. Satellite carriers must use the computer model designed by the Commission, but the Commission is not involved in making individual predictions.

If the model determines the household is "unserved" (i.e., the signal strength is too low), the satellite carrier can provide distant network signals to the household. If the model predicts that the household is served by a particular local network station over-the-air, the household is not eligible for distant signals for that network.[8] The subscriber may request waivers from each of the local stations that are predicted to serve the household in order to be eligible for distant signals.[9] Waivers are requested through the satellite carrier, and the local broadcast station must accept or reject a waiver request within 30 days. If the station does not respond to a waiver request within the time frame, the station is assumed to have agreed to the waiver.

If the local station denies the waiver request, the current law provides for a process by which the subscriber can request to have a signal test to measure the actual strength of the over-the-air signal from each station. Both the satellite and broadcast station must agree on a qualified and independent person to conduct the test. The costs of the test will be paid by either the satellite carrier or the broadcast station, depending on the outcome of the test. In limited circumstances, there are rules to provide for testing to be conducted and paid for by the subscriber directly. Others on the panel representing the affected industries can comment on whether and how often tests are requested and conducted. The Commission is not involved in the process, although we do field consumer questions about the process when requested.

Other "Unserved" Situations

The law provides that, in situations where a satellite dish is permanently affixed to a recreational vehicle or commercial truck, that subscriber is deemed to be "unserved" and eligible to receive distant signals.

Other Distant Signal Subscribers

As Congress has changed the eligibility rules for distant signals in successive reauthorizations, it has provided different treatment for subscribers to distant signals at the time of the reauthorization, depending on when the subscriber first received

---

[7] As noted below, new subscribers are not eligible for distant signals if the local-into-local package is available to them.

[8] One of the revisions added by STELA to the existing protocol was to specify that the local network signal might be available via either a so-called primary or multicast stream broadcast by a local station. This distinction was added to address the enhanced capacity associated with digital transmission, which enables stations to broadcast multiple streams of programming simultaneously.

[9] STELA revised which stations are to be considered in the predictive model so that only stations that are "local" to the consumer based on the Nielsen DMA need to be considered. Previously, all network station signals were to be considered, including those that were not treated as local for purposes of carriage.

the distant signals. These different qualifications for "grandfathering" are used to determine whether subscribers may or must take the local-into-local package if and when offered. Some of the grandfathered subscribers may keep the distant signals, others may at some point be required to relinquish the distant signals. This is a topic that has been addressed in each reauthorization process, taking into consideration equitable treatment for distant signal subscribers at the time.

Senator PRYOR. Thank you.
Senator Smith.

STATEMENT OF HON. GORDON SMITH, PRESIDENT AND CEO, NATIONAL ASSOCIATION OF BROADCASTERS

Senator SMITH. Thank you, Mr. Chair.

Thank you, Chairman Pryor, Ranking Member Wicker, members of the Committee. It's a pleasure to be back before this committee and to share with you NAB's views on STELA reauthorization.

STELA and its predecessors have achieved their intended goal of fostering satellite competition to cable monopolies and NAB feels STELA should be allowed to sunset, as Congress originally intended. However, if this committee determines that STELA should be reauthorized for another term, we support a clean bill free from controversial and unrelated provisions harmful to America's broadcasters.

As you're all well aware, the principal challenge in legislating any telecommunications matter before this committee is the rapid pace of which the industry evolves and the desire not to stand in the way of innovation, job growth, and delivery of new services to consumers. The same is true in the video marketplace.

Local television is evolving to provide viewers with the programming they crave where and when they want it. That said, now having served almost 6 years representing America's local TV broadcasters, I would like to share with you a few of the things I've learned since leaving this committee.

First, the locally-focused system of television stations in the United States is the envy of the world but it's largely taken for granted in our country. We have a system that is not regional or national, not government owned or subsidized, but one that delivers to our citizens something no other country does: local services that play a vital role in every community across this great country.

Localism underpins each of our FCC licenses and can never be replicated by broadband or by pay-TV service providers. Our stations demonstrate their commitment to this promise in times of every emergency reminding us of broadcasters' important role as first informers.

We're here to be the public's eyes and ears, to serve them during times of crisis, to share profound moments, and to connect to our families, friends and neighbors. In this era of milk and bilk and build by the bit services that stress every family's budget, our medium is free, over-the-air to all, regardless of race, creed, color, gender, or economic disposition. These Americans should not be forgotten in your deliberations.

Second, the business of broadcasting, which enables us to serve our local communities and which produces the best shows on television and delivers that content free to over-the-air viewers, has never been tougher. Today, broadcasters compete with wireless companies, pay-TV providers, over-the-top services for eyeballs, and for advertising.

To be clear, we welcome competition. It makes us better at what we do and benefits viewers regardless of how they choose to consume our highly-valued content. The truth is, local television today is sustained by only two revenue streams: by retransmission consent fees paid by those who resell our signal; and by advertising. Without this economic foundation, we could not do what we do. Localism, as a public value on our airwaves, would simply not be preserved.

Congress should resist efforts from pay-TV industry to upset the current retransmission consent framework that enables broadcasters to fulfill our fundamental mission of localism and look upon with great suspicion regulators that choose to reregulate local television's joint selling practices while turning a blind eye to pay-TV providers' joint selling practices as well. Policymakers and regulators need not intercede on behalf of the largely unregulated pay-TV industry to balance the playing field, particularly when the four top cable and satellite companies control nearly 70 percent of the video market already.

Finally, pay-TV's misinformation campaign that hypothesizes increased bills for consumers are somehow related to broadcasting is groundless. To fix this, they've offered a number of proposals, both regulatory and deregulatory, that are designed to distort what currently is a marketplace that's working. NAB will continue to oppose these efforts in Congress, at the FCC, and in the courts, if necessary.

I leave you with this plea for caution, and care in the video space and to please be mindful that unintended consequences could eliminate the benefits our country enjoys from free, local television. It's my fervent hope that this committee shares this belief and will reject haphazard, piecemeal legislative proposals proffered and supported by our competitors and our friends at this table which are specifically designed to undermine free local television.

In conclusion, please preserve the value of localism and foster a competitive video landscape. We ask you do nothing to still or jeopardize your local stations that carry your news and to leave that available to serve your public.

Thank you and I look forward to answering your questions.

[The prepared statement of Senator Smith follows:]

PREPARED STATEMENT OF HON. GORDON SMITH, PRESIDENT AND CEO, NATIONAL ASSOCIATION OF BROADCASTERS

Good afternoon, Chairman Pryor, Ranking Member Wicker and members of the Subcommittee. On behalf of the NAB and its over 1,300 local television stations, it is an honor to be back in front of this Committee.

I appreciate the opportunity to discuss the reauthorization of the Satellite Television Extension and Localism Act of 2010 (STELA), which is set to expire at the end of 2014. STELA, at its core, is a satellite bill. Passed in 1988, this law was intended to be a *temporary* fix to help satellite carriers better compete with cable. Twenty-five years later, satellite has grown to be the second and third largest pay-TV companies in America, with combined revenues of $46 billion and 34.2 million total subscribers. This law has clearly served its intended purpose, which is why NAB asks the Committee to take a hard look at whether this bill should be reauthorized at all. But, if in this Committee's wisdom it determines that STELA should receive another authorization, NAB asks that the bill be clean of any unrelated or controversial provisions that harm the ability of your local television stations to serve your local communities.

Both localism and diversity are bedrock principles that have guided communications policy for decades, and specifically the laws governing satellite carriage of broadcast signals. The key to promoting localism and diversity is the creation and distribution of locally-produced content relevant to our communities. In fact, the word "localism" even finds itself in the title of the bill we are discussing here today.

I'm proud to say that the United States does localism better than any other country around the globe. It is viewers that are rewarded with coverage of matters of importance imperative to local communities—community news, severe weather and emergency alerts, school closings, high school sports, local elections and public affairs. Localism is also support for local charities, civic organizations and community events. Broadcast stations provide local businesses a place to advertise and inform consumers about their goods and services, which in turn, creates jobs and supports local economies. It is local broadcasters that create a sense of community by addressing the needs of the public, based on a familiarity with, and commitment to, the cities and towns they serve.

For these reasons, NAB asks this Committee to continue to invest in the value of local content and keep STELA free of language that could undermine the legal framework that enables this fundamental mission of localism. While all of this is addressed in detail in the letter we provided to the Commerce Committee three weeks ago, four proposals in particular would undermine our ability to deliver locally-focused service.

First, pay-TV industry proposals that would mandate standstills or importation of distant signals in the event of retransmission consent impasses are just naked attempts to distort market-based retransmission consent negotiations in favor of cable and satellite.

In today's fiercely competitive video landscape, local broadcasters rely on the dual funding stream that comes from advertising and retransmission consent to invest in our programming. And the health of local television stations is in everyone's best interest. Broadcasters are a primary source of news and local programming. According to Pew Research, 71 percent of adults watch local television news, more than any other television news source. While you can find national news outlets on cable and the Internet, none of these channels provide the local reporting that remains so important to our democratic discourse. When cable news channels "break" stories impacting your local community, such as the tragic mudslides outside of Seattle, they use raw material provided by your local broadcasters. No other medium has boots on the ground with the experience to cover stories in a timely and accurate fashion.

The current retransmission consent system is fair given the tremendous value of the content that broadcasters provide to pay TV companies. Not only does broadcast dominate the top 100 shows on television every week, we offer the sports programming and award shows that attract the largest live audiences every year. To be fair, consumers don't buy cable to put more wires and cords in their living room or satellite to decorate the roof with an antenna; they buy these services for the content they provide. It is "must-have" broadcast programming—shows like Modern Family, New Girl, The Big Bang Theory, and NFL football—that pay-TV companies use to sell subscriptions. For this reason, it is only fair for MVPDs to pay broadcast stations for the ability to offer this value to their paying subscribers.

Attempts to paint local television stations as the behemoth in these retrans negotiations should be dismissed, since in reality it is broadcasters who are selling to a highly concentrated pay-TV market, controlled by a few large and powerful buyers. According to the recent subscriber figures, the top four pay-TV companies control 67 percent of the market. The satellite companies, who are here today asking for a leg-up in retransmission consent negotiations, make up a full one-third of all pay-TV subscribers. And the concentration among the top 10 pay-TV providers stands at 92 percent. There is no doubt, these pay-TV providers wield significant market power, yet it is the existing retransmission consent system that restores the balance of power between local television stations and highly concentrated MVPDs.

In particular, inviting the FCC to order interim carriage of a broadcast station during a dispute would assure disputes would never be resolved. Such a change would undercut the only leverage a broadcast station has to secure an agreement. Moreover, allowing pay-TV companies to import an out of market broadcast signal during a dispute—with news, weather and advertising irrelevant to those viewers—would undermine the localism Congress specifically sought to promote. It also provides a back door for MVPDs to avoid negotiating a fair rate for broadcast programming in the marketplace.

Second, reforms to the basic tier and buy-through requirements would harm our viewer's ability to access broadcast programming at a low cost. Broadcast television stations have been carried on the most highly penetrated service level by cable systems, and should remain on what's known as the "lifeline" level of service. Consumers should have access to local broadcast content like the local news, public safety, weather information and information of critical community interest. For this reason, Congress determined that broadcasters should be on the basic tier and part of every cable subscribers' package, a reason that remains important today.

The removal of broadcasters from the basic tier will have the certainly unintended effect of increasing cable bills for the subscribers who want their local broadcast channels. If taken off the basic tier, these subscribers—generally minority and elderly viewers—will be forced to buy a more expensive tier to get the programming they receive today.

Additionally, local broadcasters have concerns with MVPDs restructuring the designated market areas (DMAs) which local stations use to gauge audience share and advertising rates. While almost half of all DMAs cross state lines, local broadcasters have provided non-duplicative, local originating programming time and time again. A number of cable companies are currently providing this in-state programming and we would encourage the satellite industry to do the same.

As Congress looks at these issues, separately from the narrow STELA reauthorization, NAB believes a number of items should be considered to protect consumers from monopolistic MVPDs. No consumer should have to pay for programming they do not receive. Loss of programming from an MVPD should result in an immediate refund. Consumers should also be allowed to switch providers without prohibitive penalties. And lastly, both broadcasters and MVPDs should also keep viewers informed with enhanced consumer notifications.

Finally, I'd like to share with this Committee our serious concerns regarding the FCC's recent action on joint sales agreements and the harmful effect it will have on localism. These agreements between broadcasters, like joint ventures, foster *more* local news, provide access to capital for minority broadcasters and offer a diversity of programming options in local communities. I am so disheartened that the FCC failed to acknowledge the enormous benefits to viewers and local communities that can result from these agreements.

In conclusion, at the core of STELA and its predecessors is the fundamental concept and enduring value of broadcast localism. If the Committee decides to reauthorize STELA, NAB urges you to pass a clean reauthorization and reject calls from the pay-TV industry to add controversial issues with the sole purpose of giving them a leg up in market-based negotiations.

I thank you for your efforts and look forward to working with this Committee on a successful outcome.

Senator PRYOR. Thank you.
Mr. Palkovic.

STATEMENT OF MICHAEL W. PALKOVIC, EXECUTIVE VICE PRESIDENT, SERVICES AND OPERATIONS, DIRECTV

Mr. PALKOVIC. Thank you.

Good afternoon, Chairman Pryor, Ranking Member Wicker, and members of the Subcommittee. Thank you for inviting me to testify on STELA reauthorization and thank you and your staff for the hard work you have put in preparing for this hearing.

Last month, you sought written submissions from a variety of stakeholders. My company and DISH Network jointly submitted a response on behalf of our more than 34 million subscribers. I would like to highlight two points of that response.

First, Congress must renew STELA to preserve service to millions of your constituents. More than 1.5 million subscribers, many in rural areas of the country, receive at least one distant network signal from DirecTV or DISH. In many cases, only STELA permits them to receive network television at all. In all cases, failure to renew STELA would remove channels from people who receive them legally today, many of whom have done so for years, and who would not understand why they were taken away.

Second, when it renews STELA, Congress can also help hundreds of millions of Americans by providing blackout relief. Every time it has renewed satellite television legislation, Congress has responded to the most pressing problems of the day. Today, the biggest problem facing television viewers by far is the recent increase in broadcaster blackouts.

There were twelve blackouts in 2010. Last year, there were 127. You have now heard from both sides in what have become known as the "Retransmission Consent Wars." But your constituents do not care about who is right and wrong on these issues. They care, above all, about losing programming during broadcaster blackouts. And on this point, there is no dispute. Broadcaster blackouts have increased dramatically.

The time is ripe for some form of blackout relief. Blackout relief would not favor one side or the other. It would merely ensure that viewers don't lose the programming they depend upon. The most basic form of blackout relief would be to require broadcasters to not black out their signals. Under such a standstill provision, signals would remain up while the parties negotiate with the ultimate agreement applying retroactively so that no party benefits from delay. If parties are unable to reach agreement after some amount of time, they could submit their best-and-final offers to baseball-style arbitration.

Under another variety of blackout relief, pay-TV providers could temporarily import distant signals during broadcaster blackouts. This would be an imperfect solution, however, for consumers as they typically prefer local programming to distant programming. Yet, it would at least provide them with national network programming during disputes. Pay-TV providers would still have every incentive to reach deals with broadcasters, especially those that offer compelling local programming. And broadcasters could avoid distant signal importation simply by agreeing not to blackout their signals while negotiations are pending.

Under either form of blackout relief, consumers would no longer be held hostage during programming disputes. This is the single most important thing that Congress can do to protect hundreds of millions of Americans.

Thank you for hearing my testimony. And I look forward to your questions.

[The prepared statement of Mr. Palkovic follows:]

PREPARED STATEMENT OF MICHAEL W. PALKOVIC, EXECUTIVE VICE PRESIDENT, SERVICES & OPERATIONS, DIRECTV

Good afternoon, Chairman Rockefeller, Ranking Member Thune, Chairman Pryor, Ranking Member Wicker, and members of the Subcommittee. My name is Mike Palkovic and I am the Executive Vice President of Services and Operations of DIRECTV. Thank you for inviting me to testify on reauthorization of the Satellite Television Extension and Localism Act of 2010 (or "STELA").

I want to begin by thanking you and your staff for the hard work you have put in preparing for this hearing. Last month, you sought written submissions from a variety of stakeholders. My company and DISH Network jointly submitted a response on behalf of our more than 34 million subscribers.[1]

I would like to highlight two points of that response. *First,* Congress must renew STELA to preserve service to millions of your constituents. *Second,* when it renews STELA, Congress can also help hundreds of millions of Americans by providing "blackout relief."

With all of the other issues before this Committee, it's sometimes easy to forget that STELA's key distant signal provisions are due to expire this December. Your constituents, however, have not forgotten about these provisions.

More than 1.5 million subscribers, many in the most rural areas of the country, receive at least one distant network signal from DIRECTV or DISH. In many cases, only STELA permits them to receive network television at all. In all cases, failure to renew STELA would remove channels from people who receive them legally today—many of whom have done so for years—and who would not understand why they were taken away.

Because satellite television legislation expires every five years, however, STELA renewal also presents Congress with the opportunity to step back and examine broader issues. Congress has renewed satellite television legislation four times before. Each time, it examined intervening changes in the marketplace and acted to fix problems it found. These changes ranged from the large (permitting satellite carriers to offer local signals in 1999) to the small (updating technical provisions of the cable statutory license in 2010).[2]

Today, the biggest problem facing television viewers by far is the recent increase in broadcaster blackouts. There were twelve blackouts in 2010. Last year there were 127.

You have now heard from both sides in what have become known as the "retransmission consent wars." Broadcasters think that our subscribers don't pay them enough for their programming, even though they offer it over-the-air for free. We wish broadcasters would pay *us* for delivering their signals to millions upon millions of our subscribers who would never be able to get them over the air. We also think that outdated laws and regulations prop up broadcasters' market power, leading to all kinds of documented abuses and strong-arm tactics.

But your constituents do not care about who is right or wrong on these issues. They care above all about losing programming during broadcaster blackouts. And on this point, there is no dispute: broadcaster blackouts have increased dramatically.

Congress never meant for things to get to this point. When it passed retransmission consent in 1992, Congress meant to encourage localism. It did not mean help the big networks, and certainly did not mean to *prevent* viewers from seeing broadcast programming.

> Sen. Daniel Inouye (HI–D)—". . . If [the FCC] identifies such unforeseen instances in which a lack of agreement results in a loss of local programming to viewers, the Commission should take the regulatory steps needed to address the problem."

> Rep. Sonny Callahan (AL–R)—"This right of retransmission consent . . . is a local right. This is not, as some allege, a network bailout for Dan Rather or Jay Leno. Networks are not a party to these negotiations, except in those few instances where they own local stations themselves."

It seems clear to us, however, that changes in the marketplace over the last 20 years have swept away Congress's good intentions.

The time is ripe for some form of "blackout relief." Blackout relief would not favor one side or the other. It would merely ensure that viewers don't lose the programming they depend upon.

The most basic form of blackout relief would be to require broadcasters not to black out their signals. Under such a "standstill" provision, signals would remain up while the parties negotiate, with the ultimate agreement applying retroactively so that no party benefits from delay. If parties are unable to reach agreement after some amount of time, they could submit their best-and-final offers to baseball-style arbitration.

Under another variety of blackout relief, pay-TV providers could temporarily import distant signals during broadcaster blackouts. (Providers would pay royalties for those signals under the distant signal provisions that apply today.) This would be an imperfect solution for consumers, as they typically prefer local programming to

[1] A copy of that response is attached to this testimony as Appendix A.
[2] A chart summarizing these changes is attached to this testimony as Appendix B.

distant programming. Yet it would at least provide them with national network programming during disputes. Pay-TV providers would still have every incentive to reach deals with broadcasters, especially the handful of them that actually offer compelling local programming. And broadcasters could avoid distant signal importation simply by agreeing not to black out their signals while negotiations are pending.

Under either form of blackout relief, *consumers would no longer be held hostage during programming disputes.* This is the single most important thing that Congress can do to protect hundreds of millions of Americans.

On behalf of DIRECTV's more than 20 million subscribers, I would like to thank the Committee again for its hard work on STELA reauthorization. This bill presents challenges to the Committee. It also presents a real opportunity to make a difference. DIRECTV looks forward to working with you in the coming months to meet these challenges and to seize this opportunity.

_____

APPENDIX A—DIRECTV AND DISH NETWORK RESPONSE

Introduction and Summary

DIRECTV, LLC ("DIRECTV") and DISH Network L.L.C. ("DISH") respectfully submit these joint responses to the Committee's written questions. We applaud the Committee's bipartisan efforts to establish a broad and thoughtful discussion of pro-competition, pro-consumer reforms in concert with the reauthorization of the Satellite Television Extension and Localism Act of 2010 ("STELA").

Together, our two companies serve over 34 million pay-TV subscribers and are the second and third-largest pay-TV companies in the U.S. We also are the only respondents that: (1) serve every community in the United States, including those in the most rural areas; (2) in the case of DISH, carry every single eligible local broadcaster in all 210 designated market areas ("DMAs"); and (3) rely directly on STELA to provide service to our subscribers.

In our answers to the Committee's questions, we call upon Congress to:

- Stop local programming blackouts;
- Put an end to drastic retransmission consent rate hikes; and
- Ensure that the most rural households in the U.S. have access to the same network programming as urban and suburban households.

In support of these principles, we advocate specific measures to amend current law, including:

- Authorizing the FCC to impose baseball-style arbitration and a standstill so the programming stays up while the parties arbitrate their dispute; or, alternatively, permitting the importation of distant signals during retransmission consent disputes.
- Stipulating specific, anti-consumer actions that would fail the "good faith" requirement.
- Prohibiting joint sales agreements and other collusive methods used by broadcasters.
- Updating the definition of "unserved household" to reflect how Americans actually receive over-the-air broadcast signals today, as opposed to how they did decades ago.
- Prohibiting broadcaster blocking of online content to the broadband subscribers of a multichannel video programming distributor ("MVPD") during a dispute with that MVPD.
- Encouraging the unbundling of broadcast programming from other programming, both at the wholesale and retail levels.
- Permanently reauthorizing STELA.

The time for action is now. The current system of retransmission consent, established by Congress over 20 years ago in the 1992 Cable Act, gives each "Big Four" broadcast station a monopoly in its local market. While it may have been a fair negotiation when it was one cable company against one broadcaster, today the local broadcaster holds all of the cards and plays multiple MVPDs off of each other in any given market. Ultimately, it is the American consumer who suffers.

Broadcasters abuse their retransmission consent rights during negotiations, using brinksmanship tactics and blackouts to extract ever-greater fees from MVPDs, with no end in sight. Blackouts happen when companies like DIRECTV and DISH try to fight back and reject broadcasters' unreasonable price demands, which often involve rate increases of several hundred percent. Retransmission consent fees raised $758 million for broadcasters in 2009. They hit $3.3 billion in 2013. They are expected to reach $7.6 billion in 2019.

In 2013, there were 127 broadcaster blackouts, compared with 96 blackouts in 2012, 51 blackouts in 2011, and 12 blackouts in 2010. Thus, the number of blackouts increased over *one thousand percent* since Congress passed STELA. These numbers do not even include all of the near-misses, which are equally disruptive to the consumer experience. Compounding the injury, the timing of many blackouts coincides with marquee events like the World Series or the Oscars.

It is time for Congress to act, and STELA reauthorization presents the perfect vehicle. Every five years Congress updates the law to account for changes in the marketplace, technology, and consumer demand. It should continue to make updates and improvements to the law that will benefit consumers.

I. STELA-Specific Issues:

(1) Should Congress reauthorize STELA? If so, for how long?

Yes, permanently.

More than 1.5 million satellite subscribers—many of them in the most rural areas of the country—depend on these provisions in order to receive distant signals. Were Congress not to reauthorize STELA, these subscribers would lose access to TV service that most Americans take for granted.

Some have suggested that private licensing could take the place of STELA. That may be true under the comprehensive deregulatory approach championed in the Senate last Congress by then-Senator Jim DeMint (R–SC) and Rep. Scalise (R–LA), which would eliminate nearly all regulation of broadcast television, including the enormous regulatory benefits enjoyed by broadcasters. But nobody seriously contends that, if Congress were to eliminate STELA's *distant signal* provisions only, private licensing would replace them. Even NAB, which has opposed these provisions for decades, does not believe this.[1]

The distant signal provisions must be renewed by Congress in order for a largely rural segment of the American population to receive the same broadcast network programming as the rest of the American populace. In other words, were Congress not to renew STELA, distant signals would disappear, depriving rural Americans of a lifeline to broadcast network programming and eliminating any chance of watching a network station in "short" markets, which do not have a station affiliated with that network.

A permanent reauthorization would establish parity between satellite and cable, since the cable statutory license does not expire. We see no reason why satellite subscribers should live with the threat of losing their service when cable subscribers do not. Barring permanent reauthorization, however, Congress should extend STELA for as long as possible.

(2) Members of the Committee have heard from constituents who are unable to watch instate broadcast TV programming. Under Section 614(h) of the Communications Act, the Federal Communications Commission (FCC) has the power to modify Designated Market Areas (DMAs) for broadcast TV carriage on cable systems. Should the FCC have a similar power with respect to satellite pay TV providers to address DMA issues? Are there other ways to address these issues?

Congress should consider this solution along with others.

Satellite subscribers tell DIRECTV and DISH the same things they tell Members of Congress. They do not want to be told which "local" stations they must watch. They want choices. They also want to be able to watch news and sports that originate from within their own states.

Congress could address this issue in many ways. One legislative approach would be to permit satellite carriers to provide in-state stations to so-called "or-

---

[1] United States Copyright Office, *"Section 302" Report* at 71–72 (2011), available at *http://www.copyright.gov/reports/section302-report.pdf* ("NAB concluded that given the overwhelming economic importance to the station of appealing to viewers in its own market as opposed to cable or satellite subscribers in some distant market, there is little likelihood that stations would adjust their existing licensing models for broadcast programming specifically to accommodate the programming preferences of a distant cable operator or satellite carrier. NAB also stated that there is no incentive for a broadcaster to undertake the additional cost and administrative burden of negotiating for additional rights in order to be able to sublicense all of its station's programs to cable operators or satellite carriers serving subscribers in distant markets.") (internal citations omitted).

phan counties," which are counties that receive no in-state broadcasting. Permitting the FCC to modify DMAs holds some promise as well.

Broadcasters occasionally suggest that they can "solve" the in-state local news problem by offering private copyright licenses for local news. This, however, results in a product that consumers do not want—a "channel" that offers a blank screen for as many as 23 hours a day. We know this because DIRECTV offers such a product in Arkansas. Very few people watch it. People want to watch channels with around-the-clock programming, not blank screens.

That said, we must present two notes of caution. First, DIRECTV and DISH have each spent hundreds of millions of dollars on spot-beam satellites and ground equipment based on the Nielsen DMA boundaries. We may not be able to adjust our channel offerings to implement changes that Congress or the FCC might enact, and some of this costly capacity might have to fall into disuse.

Second, for this reason, DIRECTV and DISH urge Congress to avoid single market "fixes," as it did when it passed STELA five years ago. We can comply more easily with systematic changes than with one-off changes to individual local markets.

A general remedy proposed by DIRECTV and DISH would give subscribers the option to purchase station signals from an in-state DMA if they first receive local service. We would compensate the in-state broadcaster pursuant to the Section 119 distant signal license. To the claims from broadcasters that this would reduce local station viewership, we would note that (a) a subscriber's local stations still would be on the channel lineup, and (b) if local programming is as important and compelling as local broadcasters claim, then no material decrease in viewership should result.

(3) One of the expiring provisions in STELA is the obligation under Section 325(b) of the Communications Act for broadcast television stations and multichannel video programming distributors (MVPDs) to negotiate retransmission consent agreements "in good faith." Should the Congress modify this obligation or otherwise clarify what it means to negotiate retransmission consent in good faith? If so, how?

Yes. Congress should clarify and expand the "good faith" rules.

Congress has already instructed the FCC to adopt and enforce rules that "prohibit a television broadcast station that provides retransmission consent from . . . failing to negotiate in good faith."[2] Such rules are supposed to provide that a broadcaster violates its good faith duty when its demands include terms or conditions not based on competitive marketplace considerations.[3] In implementing this mandate, the FCC has created a two-prong standard: a list of specific acts and practices that are *per se* a violation of good faith, and a totality of the circumstances test.[4] While the second prong—the totality of the circumstances—gives the agency some flexibility to consider broader types of anticompetitive conduct that we have observed, to date it has not been used in this way. Moreover, the FCC has interpreted the law as not contemplating an "intrusive role" for the agency.[5] As a result, the FCC has never found a violation of the good faith requirement.

Broadcasters plainly do not consider the good faith rules an impediment to their behavior. In such circumstances, it should surprise no one that broadcaster blackouts are accelerating and retransmission consent fees are increasing at an alarming rate, driving up consumer prices.

Congress should thus clarify and expand the good faith requirement. At a minimum, the requirement should prohibit the following:

- Brinkmanship tactics, such as threatening programming blackouts designed to exploit a network-affiliated broadcast station's already substantial market power. (We discuss ideas for "blackout relief" below in response to Question II.1.b.1.)
- Withholding of retransmission consent from an MVPD without granting that provider relief to permit importation of same-network distant signals through-

---

[2] 47 U.S.C. § 325(b)(3)(C)(ii).
[3] *Id.*
[4] 47 C.F.R. § 76.65(b)(1)–(2).
[5] *Amendment of the Commission's Rules Related to Retransmission Consent,* 26 FCC Rcd. 2718, ¶ 20 (2011).

out the market until a carriage agreement has been reached.[6] (This also falls within our discussion of "blackout relief.")

- Giving a network the right to negotiate or approve a station's retransmission consent agreements or any major term in such agreements. (We discuss joint retransmission consent negotiation in more detail below in response to Question II.1.b.ii.)

- Granting another non-commonly owned station or station group the right to negotiate or approve a station's retransmission consent agreements. (We discuss joint retransmission consent negotiation in more detail below in response to Question II.1.b.ii.).

- Demanding that an MVPD not carry legally available out-of-market stations (*e.g.,* distant signals or significantly viewed signals), or substantially burdening such carriage, as a condition of retransmission consent.

- Deauthorizing carriage immediately prior to or during marquee events, such as the Super Bowl, World Series, or Academy Awards. (We discuss the so-called "sweeps provisions" in more detail below in response to Question II.1.b.v.)

- Refusing to give a stand-alone offer for retransmission consent when requested by an MVPD, or giving a stand-alone offer so high as to not constitute a *bona fide* offer. (We discuss stand-alone offers in more detail below in response to Question II.1.b.vi.)

- Imposing a blackout in any DMA where the broadcaster has failed to provide an adequate over-the-air signal to a materially large number of subscribers.

None of these activities ought to be considered consistent with "competitive marketplace considerations." None should be permitted under the good faith standard.

(4) As part of STELA, Congress changed the statutory standard by which households are determined to be "unserved" by broadcast TV signals. Does Congress or the FCC need to take further action to implement this previous legislative amendment?

Yes, further action is necessary. For years, the law specified that households would be considered "served" (and thus ineligible for distant signals) if tested or predicted to receive signals of a specified strength using a "conventional, stationary, outdoor rooftop receiving antenna."[7] (Since the antenna is supposed to be pointed at each station tested, this really means a "rotating" antenna, not a "stationary" one.) But most Americans do not have rooftop antennas and have not for many decades. People today use indoor antennas. We have consistently argued that the relevant standard should reflect the kinds of equipment actually deployed in the marketplace.[8]

Moreover, just before the digital transition, the FCC ruled that broadcasters did not have to replicate their analog "Grade B" signal coverage areas with the new, digital broadcast signal contours, increasing the number of households that cannot receive an over-the-air signal using a typical indoor digital antenna.

In response, Congress changed the relevant statutory criteria to refer simply to an "antenna."[9] Congress removed all prior specifications—"conventional," "stationary," "outdoor," and "rooftop."

We believe that Congress intended to permit use of indoor antennas as part of the standard. This certainly was our understanding at the time, based on our conversations with Members of Congress and Congressional staff.

---

[6] For satellite carriers, such relief would take the form of waivers to the "no-distant-where-local" and "unserved household" rules. 47 U.S.C. §§ 339(a)(2)(E), (c)(2). For cable operators, such relief would take the form of waivers of the network nonduplication and syndicated exclusivity rules. 47 C.F.R. § 76.92 *et seq.*

[7] 17 U.S.C. § 119(d)(10)(A) (2004).

[8] *See, e.g.,* Letter from DIRECTV, Inc. and DISH Network, L.L.C., FCC EB Docket No. 06–94, (filed Nov. 4, 2010) (providing CEA figures related to antenna purchases as part of technical submission); *Satellite Delivery of Network Signals to Unserved Households for Purposes of the Satellite Home Viewer Act,* 14 FCC Rcd. 2654, ¶ 52 (1999) (citing comments of satellite providers urging an indoor antenna standard, but citing to then-current statutory language specifying the use of outdoor rooftop antennas).

[9] 17 U.S.C. § 119(d)(10)(A).

The FCC, however, did not construe the deletions in that manner, and decided to leave the "outdoor rooftop" criteria unchanged in its rules.[10] Thus, the predictive model and test still assume use of equipment that almost nobody uses.

This means that satellite subscribers in rural areas often can be left without access to broadcast network programming. If, for whatever reason, a satellite carrier does not offer a local station, the subscriber often can get no network service at all. She cannot receive local signals because she is too far from the transmitter. And we cannot give her distant signals because the FCC test thinks she can receive local signals.

This occurs far more often than one might think. Last summer, DIRECTV conducted nearly 1,800 signal tests in three local markets, and compared those results to the FCC's predictive model that is intended to predict whether people can receive local signals. As many as *two-thirds* of those predicted to receive local signals could not actually receive a viewable picture—and this was using a rooftop antenna. If it had been able to conduct indoor antenna tests, the figures would undoubtedly have been much worse still.

We thus believe that Congress should mandate a change to the standard and give the FCC more unequivocal direction than was issued in STELA.

(5) Are there other technical issues in STELA that have arisen since its passage in 2010 that should be addressed in the current reauthorization?

No.

II. General Video Policy Issues

(1) Some have suggested that Congress adopt structural changes to the retransmission consent system established under Section 325 of the Communications Act (Act). Others have indicated that the retransmission consent system is working as Congress intended when it was developed as part of the Cable Television Consumer Protection and Competition Act of 1992.

(a) Should Congress adopt reforms to retransmission consent? If so, what specific reforms could best protect consumers? If not, why not?

Yes. The retransmission consent rules date from 1992—the same year *Wayne's World* was released, AT&T introduced the first video phone (for $1,500), and the Washington Redskins won their last Super Bowl.

The video marketplace has changed beyond recognition since then. But regulation of the retransmission consent regime has not.

In particular, when Congress created the retransmission consent regime in 1992, it sought to balance the market power of monopoly cable operators against the monopoly power of broadcast network affiliates with exclusive territories. In the ensuing two decades, however, the video programming distribution industry has undergone profound changes. While cable operators still have market power, they are not monopolies in the markets for video distribution. Most consumers can now choose from among three or more distributors—not to mention online video providers. But *broadcasters'* exclusive territories and the Commission's retransmission consent regime have remained largely unchanged.

Moreover, broadcasters have increasingly engaged in conduct designed to enhance their bargaining power even beyond what they possessed in 1992. This includes collusion in the negotiation of retransmission consent (we describe this in more detail below in response to Question II.1.b.ii, regarding joint retransmission consent negotiation) and prohibiting the use of their programming as a distant network or significantly viewed station, even though the law allows it.

---

[10] *Measurement Standards for Digital Television Signals Pursuant to the Satellite Home Viewer Extension & Reauthorization Act of 2004*, 25 FCC Rcd. 16471 (2010) ("*2010 Measurement Order*"). The FCC reasoned: "the change in statutory language simply affords that Commission latitude to consider all types of antennas." *Id.*, ¶ 12. It concluded that an outdoor antenna was the more appropriate standard because (1) it "has always assumed" that people who could not receive a signal using an indoor antenna would employ an outdoor one; (2) the stations' service contours themselves were developed assuming the use of outdoor antennas; and (3) it believed that no reliable method for indoor testing had then been developed. *Id.*, ¶ 12–14. We are aware of no evidence to support the FCC's first "assumption." The FCC's latter two arguments have nothing to do with whether subscribers actually use outdoor antennas or not. Indeed, the FCC itself noted: "[W]e remain aware and concerned that using the outdoor measurement procedures may result in instances where a consumer who either cannot use an outdoor antenna or cannot receive service using an outdoor antenna and is not able to receive a station's service with an indoor antenna will be found ineligible for satellite delivery of a distant network signal." *Id.*, ¶ 21.

Broadcasters have exploited this situation by abusing their retransmission consent rights during negotiations, using the tactics of brinksmanship and blackouts to extract ever-greater fees from MVPDs—this is an escalating problem with no end in sight. SNL Kagan estimates that MVPDs paid $3.3 billion in retransmission consent fees in 2013, and that this figure will soar to a staggering $7.6 billion by 2019.

When MVPDs decline to meet broadcaster's demands, they face the loss of programming for their subscribers. In 2013, there were 127 broadcaster blackouts, compared with 96 blackouts in 2012, 51 blackouts in 2011, and 12 blackouts in 2010.

The result? Consumers are harmed no matter what the MVPD chooses. Either the MVPD acquiesces, in which case subscribers pay higher prices for programming. Or the MVPD resists, in which case the subscriber loses key programming. Consumers also may be forced by blackouts to switch from their first choice provider. This, in turn, can cause the loss of their chosen package, pricing, and DVR recording history, not to mention the hassle of transferring billing, equipment and set up to their second (or third) choice provider. Broadcaster blackouts, moreover, affect all MVPDs. Thus, a consumer who switches MVPDs in order to obtain broadcast programming may find herself needing to do so again within a short time.

As DISH has noted previously, rural households suffer disproportionately from broadcaster blackouts.[11] Moreover, broadcasters in many cases simply have failed to provide an adequate over-the-air signal to reach many rural communities. As discussed above in more detail below in response to Question I.4, DIRECTV has found that as many as two-thirds of those predicted to receive local signals could not actually receive a viewable picture.

Examples of Communities Underserved by Big Four Broadcast Station Signal [12]

DMA	Community Affected	"Big Four" Digital Broadcast Signals Received	Missing "Big Four" Networks
Denver, CO	Steamboat Springs, CO	None	ABC, CBS, FOX, NBC
Fargo-Valley City, ND	Cavalier, ND	WDAZ–TV (ABC); KNRR (FOX)	CBS, NBC
Medford-Klamath Falls, OR	Lakeview, OR	KOTI (NBC)	ABC, CBS, FOX
New York, NY	Ellenville, NY	WRGB (CBS)	ABC, FOX, NBC
Phoenix, AZ	Globe, AZ	KPNX (NBC); KPHO-TV (CBS)	ABC, FOX
Spokane, WA	Lewiston, ID	KLEW–TV (CBS); KHQ-TV (NBC)	ABC, FOX

Clearly, then, Congress should act.

We discuss the six proposals cited by the Committee, along with several others, immediately below. (Please note that we discussed some of these reforms in the context of the FCC's "good faith negotiation" rules above in response to Question I.3.)

(b) Please comment on the following possible reforms that have been suggested by various parties:

(i) Providing the FCC authority to order interim carriage of a broadcast signal or particular programming carried on such signal (and the circumstances under which that might occur).

We strongly support this proposal. We think of this idea as one form of "blackout relief" for subscribers. It strikes us as the single most important thing Congress could do in the STELA reauthorization.

One can agree with the MVPD in a particular retransmission consent fight. Or one can agree with the broadcaster. But we should all be able to agree that the *subscriber* should not be put in the middle. Subscribers have done nothing wrong. All they want is to watch television from the MVPD that they have chosen.

---

[11] *See* Comments of DISH Network, MB Dkt. No. 10–71 at 11–14 (filed May 27, 2011). These comments, along with the Comments of DIRECTV, LLC, MB Dkt. No. 10–71 (filed May 27, 2011) ("DIRECTV Retransmission Consent Comments") are attached hereto as Exhibit B.
[12] *Id.* at 13.

Blackout relief would let them do just that. It would require the FCC to order interim carriage during all blackouts. And it would provide that subsequent agreements will govern carriage back to the date of the blackout, so neither party is advantaged by the interim carriage.

Better yet would be to combine interim carriage with baseball-style arbitration. This would keep the programming up so consumers do not suffer, and ensure that the broadcasters are fairly compensated through a formal arbitration process.

Blackout relief works best if it is mandatory and applies automatically. Asking the FCC to order interim carriage during *some* blackouts would be costly and time consuming, and would inappropriately put the focus on the behavior of MVPDs and broadcasters, when the focus should be on the harm caused to the consumer.

Blackout relief could also take the form of changes to the distant signal rules. Congress should permit (or direct the FCC to permit) pay TV providers to deliver distant signals during blackouts. While less perfect than full interim carriage, this distant signal fix would allow us to provide subscribers with an imperfect substitute during a local broadcaster's blackout, thereby softening the blow to consumers. Subscribers in such circumstances would continue to have access to a network affiliate but would not have local news, weather and sports.

For example, if a broadcaster were to black out the local Charleston-Huntington, West Virginia FOX station, DIRECTV and DISH would be able to temporarily bring in an out-of-market station, such as the Lexington, Kentucky FOX station (with the MVPD paying the compulsory copyright fee for each subscriber). The replacement station would not be a perfect substitute for the blacked-out local station, since consumers would not have their local content, but at least some measure of protection would be extended to affected consumers by providing access to network programming. Additionally, this fix would level the playing field a bit in the negotiating process and make it more likely that the broadcaster would not pull its signal in the first place. Broadcasters would be introduced to some of the same competitive pressures that satellite carriers and cable operators face every day, and consumers would benefit as a result.

These forms of blackout relief would not "interfere" with the "free market," as broadcasters have argued, for the simple reason that the market is not free; it is skewed by the legal monopolies and regulatory benefits enjoyed by the four networks. The retransmission consent "marketplace" is one littered with invasive government rules that favor broadcasters and disfavor MVPD subscribers. A list of these appears as Exhibit A. Every single one of these rules gives special privileges to broadcasters. These privileges do not apply to pay-TV networks (such as CNN or ESPN), Internet programming, or any other kind of video product other than broadcasting.

In today's highly regulated market, however, broadcasters cannot reasonably object to protecting subscribers through blackout relief.

If Congress truly believes that broadcasters are special, and that there should be a "social contract between the government and broadcasters to serve the 'public interest' (*e.g.,* provide 'local' programming and a 'diversity of voices' to as many Americans as possible)," [13] it should ensure that consumers do not lose the benefit of this bargain.

(ii) Prohibiting joint retransmission consent negotiations for multiple TV stations at the same time.

Of all the reforms presented to Congress, this should be the easiest to implement.

Broadcasters should not be able to evade FCC rules through legal tricks. Yet this is exactly what broadcasters are doing today.

The FCC's media ownership rules generally prohibit one entity from owning more than one "big four" network affiliate in a market.[14] And they generally

---

[13] Phoenix Center, *"An Economic Framework for Retransmission Consent,"* Policy Paper No. 47 at 1 (Dec. 2013).

[14] 47 C.F.R. § 73.3555(b).

prohibit excessive concentration of broadcast ownership across markets.[15] Thus, collusive joint retransmission consent negotiation should already be prohibited.

Broadcasters, however, increasingly evade these rules through "sidecar" arrangements such as JSAs, SSAs, and similar endeavors. DIRECTV's own internal records show that in nearly half of the markets in which it carries local signals, it must negotiate with a party controlling multiple affiliates of the "Big Four" networks. This does not even count the increasing practice of networks insisting on negotiating or approving retransmission consent on behalf of their allegedly independent affiliates.

Nobody carries more broadcasters than DIRECTV and DISH. We can assure you that these sidecar arrangements harm viewers. They lead to higher prices (as much as 161 percent higher, according to one estimate).[16] And they by definition cause greater harm when blackouts occur.

This is why the Department of Justice recently submitted a filing at the FCC that highlighted the harms of these tactics and urged the FCC to require the broadcast ownership rules to treat any two stations participating in such an arrangement as being under common ownership.[17] DOJ found that, "[g]iven the extensive control over pricing decisions inherent" in such arrangements, they should be attributable under the FCC's ownership rules.[18] And it stated that "failure to treat JSAs and similar arrangements as attributable interests could provide opportunities for parties to circumvent any competitive purposes of the multiple ownership limits." [19]

The FCC Chairman recently proposed to generally prohibit joint retransmission consent negotiations between non-commonly owned stations. The House Commerce Committee's discussion STELA reauthorization draft contains a similar approach.

We support both of these proposals. Some broadcasters point to instances in which SSAs and JSAs have led to more local news, or joint ownership of a news helicopter, or other public goods. We do not object to such arrangements. Our primary concern is when broadcasters collude on *external* functions—particularly retransmission consent.

Other broadcasters say that they need to negotiate retransmission consent on behalf of more stations in order to ensure their continued ability to offer local news and information. If they really believe this, they should make the case to Congress and the FCC to relax the ownership limits. Unless and until they do so, they should not be allowed to rely on legal tricks to evade the Commission's rules and harm consumers.

Finally, although the Committee does not ask this question directly, the retransmission consent problems reflect a larger pattern of network dominance over affiliates in the broadcast markets. DIRECTV, for example, has argued that network "rights of refusal" or even outright negotiation on behalf of "independent" affiliates should be considered attributable under the FCC's ownership rules and violations of its good faith rules.[20]

As part of STELA reauthorization, Members of the Committee might ask their local broadcasters:

- Do you think your network has demanded too much control over retransmission consent negotiations and programming time?
- Do you think too much of your station's retransmission consent fees are sent back to network headquarters rather than to your local station to support local news, weather, sports, and public affairs programming?

---

[15] *Id.* § 73.3555(e).

[16] William P. Rogerson, *Coordinated Negotiation of Retransmission Consent Agreements by Separately Owned Broadcasters in the Same Market* (May 27, 2011), filed as an attachment to the Comments of American Cable Association, MB Docket No. 10–71 (filed May 27, 2011); William P. Rogerson, *Joint Control or Ownership of Multiple Big Four Broadcasters in the Same Market and Its Effect on Retransmission Consent Fees,* MB Docket No. 10–71 (May 18, 2010), filed as an attachment to the Comments of the American Cable Association, MB Docket No. 10–71 (filed May 18, 2010).

[17] *Ex Parte* Submission of the United States Department of Justice, MB Docket Nos. 09–182, 07–294, and 04–256 (filed Feb. 20, 2014).

[18] *Id.* at 15–16.

[19] *Id.* at 16 (internal citations omitted).

[20] DIRECTV Retransmission Consent Comments at 19.

We believe that candid answers to these questions would stand in contrast to NAB's claim that the current retransmission consent system does not require reform.

(iii) Mandating refunds for consumers in the case of a programming blackout (and apportioning the ultimate responsibility for the cost of such refunds).

Mandatory refunds would not be pro-consumer as they might result in the elimination of current consumer benefits and flexibility.

The proposal stems from broadcast claims that subscribers cannot switch providers during blackouts because long-term satellite service agreements impose "early termination fees." This, however, is only half of the story.

To begin with, DIRECTV and DISH subscribers are never required to enter into a service agreement. They can *choose* to do so if they would like to lower the up—front cost of equipment and installation. Alternatively, they can pay the full cost of equipment and installation when they commence service and enter into no service commitment.

We offer service agreements because we invest as much as $1,000 to provide service to a new residential subscriber. This includes the full-price of installation and equipment. Subscribers choose service agreements because it makes more sense for them to pay these costs over the long term than all at once.

And every service agreement clearly states that programming and channel line-ups are subject to change and are not cause for either party to end the agreement.

Were Congress to mandate refunds during blackouts, we would find ourselves less able to offer long-term service agreements. This, in turn, would force subscribers to pay the full price of equipment and installation up front.

Such a measure would only serve to increase broadcaster leverage in retransmission disputes, when the scales are already so tipped in their favor. This would make such disputes more common. And it would lead broadcasters to demand even higher prices.

Perhaps broadcasters would agree to amending the law so that any broadcaster that blacks out its signal during a retransmission consent dispute must credit all impacted subscribers with the amount of retransmission consent fees paid retroactively to the broadcaster during that period. This might: deter the broadcaster from blacking out its programming in the first place; incent the broadcaster to reach an agreement quickly when it does black out a signal; and offer some financial compensation subscribers who lose service through no fault of their own. DIRECTV and DISH would gladly credit the full amount of such restitution to subscribers upon receipt from the broadcaster.

(iv) Prohibiting a broadcast television station from blocking access to its online content, that is otherwise freely available to other Internet users, for an MVPD's subscribers while it is engaged in a retransmission consent negotiation with that MVPD.

This, too, is a wise reform, as illustrated by the fact that CBS recently blocked access to online content by Time Warner Cable's broadband subscribers nationwide during the retransmission dispute between the two. Such blocking harms MVPD video subscribers in the same way that blackouts harm them more generally. But it also harms others. Some people have no MVPD video service and rely on the broadband connection to get video content. Others get video from one provider and broadband from another. Yet they can be caught up in a dispute and denied Internet content even though they actually are still paying for a video service that includes the broadcaster's signal.

Congress should prohibit such conduct outright. At a minimum, it should clarify that website blocking against such viewers constitutes a *per se* violation of the good faith rules.

(v) Eliminating the "sweeps" exception that prevents MVPDs from removing broadcast TV channels during a sweeps period, or alternatively extending that exception to prevent broadcasters from withholding their signals or certain programming carried on such signals under certain circumstances.

To begin with, neither DIRECTV nor DISH has ever blacked out broadcast TV channels. Broadcasters black out channels by withholding consent.

This fix constitutes a matter of fairness and creates parity between MVPDs and broadcasters. One could imagine a fair set of retransmission consent rules containing no restrictions on the timing of disputes. (The DeMint/Scalise approach does this, as does the House Energy and Commerce Committee discussion draft.)

Even better from a consumer perspective would be a prohibition on blackouts both during sweeps weeks (which are important to broadcasters) and prior to and during marquee events such as the Super Bowl, World Series, or Academy Awards (all of which are important to viewers and have been used at one time or another by broadcasters as leverage to receive higher fees). Such a rule could be formulated both by referencing a limited number of specific events or in terms of ratings or some other parallel metric.

Under the existing formulation, however, the government protects only one side's economic interests—the broadcasters'. This ultimately harms consumers, and certainly has no place in allegedly "free market" negotiations.

(vi) Prohibiting retransmission consent agreements that are conditioned on the carriage by an MVPD of non-broadcast programming or non-broadcast channels of programming affiliated with the broadcast license holder.

Congress should prohibit the *forced* tying (whether explicit or *de facto*) of affiliated content as a condition of gaining access to a station's signal. It should not prohibit all *offers* of bundled programming.

Forced tying most often arises in negotiations with the large station groups affiliated with national networks, which use their "must have" broadcast programming as negotiating leverage to gain carriage for new and/or unpopular cable channels affiliated with the corporate parent.

Refusal to even discuss carriage of the station's Big Four network signal separately from carriage of other tied programming introduces an additional element of cost and complexity to the negotiation, and thereby increases the risk that the parties will reach an impasse. Such an outcome does not serve the public interest.

To be clear, we are not saying that Congress should prohibit all offers that bundle retransmission consent with carriage of additional content. Indeed, in many cases, we have found the terms and conditions of a bundled offer attractive. If, however, an MVPD requests an offer for retransmission consent on a stand-alone basis, there is no reason why the broadcaster should refuse to honor that request.

In order to be effective, such a rule would have to distinguish between *bona fide* and sham offers for stand-alone programming. We do not think this would be difficult to police in practice. A demand for significant price increases over the prior agreement if the distributor purchases retransmission on a stand-alone basis would be an example of a sham offer.

The FCC has a similar remedy with respect to stand-alone broadband offerings by Comcast in connection with the Comcast/NBCU merger. There, the FCC required Comcast to offer stand-alone broadband service "at reasonable market-based prices" and "on equivalent terms and conditions" to the most comparable bundled offering.[21]

(2) Should Congress maintain the rule that cable subscribers must buy the broadcast channels in their local market as part of any cable package? If the rule is eliminated, should an exception be made for non-commercial stations?

We are not cable operators and are not subject to this requirement.

(3) Should Congress maintain the rule that cable systems include retransmission consent stations on their basic service tiers?

We are not cable operators and are not subject to this requirement.

(4) Section 623 of the Act allows rate regulation of cable systems unless the FCC makes an affirmative finding of "effective competition." Should Congress maintain, modify, or eliminate these provisions?

We are not cable operators and are not subject to this requirement.

(5) Should Congress repeal the set-top box integration ban? If Congress repeals the integration ban, should Congress take other steps to ensure competition in the set-top box marketplace both today and in the future?

We are not cable operators and are not subject to this requirement.

---

[21] *Comcast Corp., General Electric Co., and NBC Universal, Inc.* 26 FCC Rcd. 4238, app. A, § IV.D (2011).

(6) Should Congress limit the use of shared services agreements (SSAs) and joint sales agreements (JSAs) by broadcast television ownership groups, and if so, under what circumstances?

Please see our response to question II.b.ii, in which we discuss such arrangements in the context of joint retransmission consent negotiations.

(7) Should Congress act in response to concerns that the increasing cost of video programming is the main cause behind the consistent rise in pay TV rates and that programming contracts contribute to the lack of consumer choice over programming packages? If so, what actions can it take?

From our perspective, this question sets forth the very impetus for retransmission consent reform—skyrocketing broadcaster price increases resulting in more and more disputes and blackouts and higher rates for our subscribers. As described in our response to Question II.2.b.vi, moreover, we believe that the very worst instances of tying involve broadcast programming.

Programming costs are the single largest input cost for both DIRECTV and DISH. They cost even more than the satellites we use to provide our services. As such, they have a direct impact on what subscribers pay for service.

Of course, we are concerned about price increases and tying for *all* programming, not just broadcast programming. But, as described above, broadcast prices have increased much faster than those for any other type of programming—even sports programming.

We think broadcast programming has become the most problematic kind of programming because only broadcast programming is subject to a thicket of government rules that favor one side over the other. Moreover, STELA itself relates to broadcast programming. While we welcome Congressional efforts to control runaway programming prices more broadly, it makes sense to focus on the most acute problems in the video marketplace as part of STELA reauthorization.

(8) With consumers increasingly watching video content online, should Congress extend existing competitive protections for the traditional television marketplace to the online video marketplace? If so, what types of protections?

We are still analyzing whether Congress should extend existing competitive protections for the traditional television marketplace to the online video marketplace, and have not yet formulated an opinion on this.

(9) The Consumer Choice in Online Video Act, S. 1680, is one approach to fostering a consumer-centric online video marketplace. Are there elements of that bill that should be considered in conjunction with the STELA reauthorization?

S. 1680 contains several provisions helpful to consumers. In particular, provisions prohibiting Internet blocking during retransmission consent disputes could be beneficial. So would the provisions encouraging broadcasters and upstream copyright holders to provide copyright licensing for online delivery.

On the other hand, several provisions appear to impose additional, unwarranted regulation on MVPDs. One such provision would prohibit many exclusive arrangements—even those between distributors without market power and unaffiliated programmers. Such arrangements have enabled both of our companies to compete against cable operators that still maintain dominant market share in most of America.

(10) Would additional competition for broadband and consumer video services be facilitated by extending current pole attachment rights to broadband service providers that are not also traditional telecommunications or cable providers?

Our two companies do not use pole attachments at this time but, as stated above, we generally support regulatory parity.

(11) Would additional competition for broadband and consumer video services be facilitated by extending a broadcaster's carriage rights for a period of time if they relinquish their spectrum license as part of the FCC's upcoming incentive auction?

We generally support efforts to facilitate the most spectrum possible made available in the incentive auctions. That said, we think that broadcast carriage rights should not be *expanded* as part of any incentive auction.

(12) Are there other video policy issues that the Congress should take up as part of its discussions about the STELA reauthorization?

We are unaware of any such issues at this time, other than as noted above.

APPENDIX B—HISTORY OF THE SATELLITE HOME VIEWER ACT AND AMENDMENTS

A BRIEF HISTORY OF THE SATELLITE HOME VIEWER ACT

1. Satellite Home Viewer Act of 1988, Pub. L. No. 100–667 ("SHVA")

- Created distant signal statutory license. (17 U.S.C. § 119)
- Limited distant signal service to "unserved" households—defined as households that, among other things, had not subscribed to a cable system within the previous 90 days.

2. Satellite Home Viewer Act of 1994, Pub. L. No. 103–369 ("SHVA")

- Created "challenge" procedures for networks to dispute eligibility of households, and measurement procedures for satellite carriers to demonstrate eligibility.
- Created "loser pays" formulation for signal measurement.

3. Satellite Home Viewer Improvement Act of 1999, Pub L. No. 106–113, App. I. ("SHVIA")

- Created new statutory license for local into local transmissions. (17 U.S.C. § 122)
- Created Communications Act "carry-one, carry-all" rules for satellite. (47 U.S.C. § 338)
- Subjected satellite local carriage to retransmission consent. (47 U.S.C. § 325)
- Created Communications Act distant signal rules. (47 U.S.C. § 339)
- Changed definition of "unserved household" in distant signal license to remove reference to cable subscription.
- Created waiver process by which local stations could permit distant signals to be delivered to houses otherwise ineligible.
- Created rules governing distant signal eligibility based on predictive model and measurement, replacing prior "challenge" procedure.
- Created "C-band" and "Grade B doughnut" exemptions permitting distant signal service to a limited number of longtime subscribers.
- Created RV and Truck eligibility.
- Permitted carriage of national PBS feed.
- Conditioned copyright license on compliance with FCC carriage rules.
- Subjected satellite carriage of distant signals to sports blackout rules.
- Subjected satellite carriage of nationally distributed superstations to syndicated exclusivity and network nonduplication rules.
- Created extensive complaint procedure for allegations of provisions of distant signals to ineligible subscribers.

4. Satellite Home Viewer Extension and Reauthorization Act of 2004, Pub. L. No. 108–447 ("SHVERA")

- Permitted satellite carriage of "significantly viewed" signals.
- Created "no-distant-where-local" formulation, including separate waiver provisions.
- Created license for limited local retransmission of low-power TV signals.
- Permitted carriage of non-network stations in commercial establishments.
- Created privacy rights for satellite subscribers corresponding to those that had applied to cable subscribers.
- Prohibited "two-dish" arrangement under which DISH required subscribers to obtain second satellite dish to see lesser-viewed local stations.
- Created special rules requiring carriage of all local signals in Alaska, and prohibiting out-of-state distant signals in Alaska.
- Provided for expedited DOJ consideration of voluntary agreements to provide local carriage in additional markets.
- Permitted carriage of distant and local digital signals, and created separate "digital white area."
- Created special exemptions for carriage of in-state signals in certain markets.
- Created "testing waivers" under which satellite could not deliver distant digital signals to stations experiencing problems completing the digital transition.

- Permitted satellite carriers to rely entirely on predictive modeling and to refuse to engage in on-site testing, other than at the subscriber's request and expense.

5. Satellite Television Extension and Localism Act of 2010, Pub L. No. 111–175 ("STELA")

- Reinstated distant signal license to DISH Network (which had lost the right to provide such service under the so-called "death penalty" provisions) upon verification of DISH's service of all 210 local markets.
- Eliminated "Grade B Bleed" by defining "unserved household" restriction based on off-air reception of *in market stations only.*
- Prohibited distant signal service to those who can receive local *multicast* signals off-air (with complex implementation phase-in).
- Harmonized "no-distant-where-local" rules to combine prior analog-and digital-specific rules.
- Prohibited discrimination in carriage of high definition public television stations.
- Required FCC to develop predictive model for digital signals.
- Increased statutory damages for distant signal violations tenfold.
- Permitted carriage of low-power stations throughout local market.
- Permitted distant signal carriage of networks of public stations.
- Modified cable statutory license to resolve several technical problems that had arisen over the years, including carriage of multicast streams.
- Directed Copyright Office to initiate filing fees.
- Directed Copyright Office to permit audits of statements of account.
- Directed FCC, Copyright office, GAO to issue six reports collectively.

Senator PRYOR. Thank you.
Mr. Powell.

STATEMENT OF HON. MICHAEL K. POWELL, PRESIDENT AND CHIEF EXECUTIVE OFFICER, NATIONAL CABLE & TELECOMMUNICATIONS ASSOCIATION

Mr. POWELL. Good afternoon, Mr. Chairman and members of the Subcommittee. My name is Michael Powell and I have the privilege of being the President and CEO of NCTA. Thank you for inviting me today to offer our thoughts on the reauthorization of STELA and I'm pleased to be here.

Mr. Chairman, we fully support the reauthorization of STELA and particularly the provision that requires broadcasters and MVPDs to negotiate in good faith when conducting retransmission consent negotiations. Good faith is more important than ever. With the stresses of retransmission consent negotiations and blackouts, it is vital that the Committee ensure that this bilateral legal obligation remains part of the retransmission consent regime.

We also support additional reforms that are appropriate and overdue given the competitive realities of today's video marketplace. And we deeply appreciate the Committee's willingness to consider them.

NCTA has identified three narrow yet very important reforms that would prune away outdated legal requirements directly benefiting consumers and promoting a more level playing field among competing providers of multichannel video services.

First, NCTA supports repeal of the FCC's integration ban which forces only cable operators and not other MVPDs to include a separate video decryption component in the leased set-top box. Congress intended, as part of the 1996 Act, to create the conditions for a retail market for set-top boxes. To implement the law, the FCC had to overcome the obstacle giving third-party boxes access to encrypted signals. Industry worked together to create the CableCARD so boxes could be sold, unlocked at retail, and work in any cable market simply by requiring a card.

The FCC, however, stepped beyond the statute and imposed the integration ban. The ban forced cable companies to place security functions out of their leased boxes and rely, instead, on CableCARDs even though there's no technical need to do so and consumers would not enjoy any additional features or benefits. The theory of the rule was behavioral. The belief that cable companies would have the incentive to support CableCARDs for third parties if they had to use them and thereby help seed what they hoped to be a flourishing retail market for set-top boxes. Despite its merits; it has not had its intended effect.

We now see that, while CableCARDs are a fully realized solution, the integration ban has not stimulated a consumer appetite for third-party devices. Today, over 45 million leased boxes are using CableCARDs while a mere 600,000 have been requested for retail devices. The explosion of unimagined video devices and content sources from companies like Netflix, Amazon, Roku, and a wealth of Apple and Android devices, likely explaining the lessening appetite among consumers for alternative set-top boxes. Yet, consumers that choose a cable operator's leased box are paying a penalty in unnecessary expense and energy cost.

Recent evidence filed with the FCC just last year by one large cable operator seeking a waiver, indicated the cost of including CableCARD and current set-top boxes is between $40 and $50. We estimate that the cost attributable to the integration ban has exceeded a billion dollars for the industry. And, based on EPA figures, subscribers collectively foot the bill for over 500 million kilowatts of unnecessary energy consumed by CableCARDs.

Second, while we take no position on the propriety of Joint Advertising or Shared Service Agreements, we do support the legislative effort to prohibit broadcasters from engaging in joint negotiations with cable operators and other MVPDs for retransmission consent. Through a variety of agreements, certain broadcasters have been increasing their leverage in the negotiations by banding together, despite being competitors, and negotiating as a single entity rather than separately. The DOJ and the FCC have raised significant concerns about these anticompetitive practices, and it's appropriate for Congress to address this issue as a complement to actions taken recently by the FCC.

Third, we support eliminating the must-buy requirement for stations that freely elect to negotiate the price and terms of their carriage. Having chosen the free market in pursuit of top-dollar, these stations should not enjoy a government guarantee that assures they're carried on the basic tier and forces consumers to purchase their channels as a prerequisite to buying any other programming package. Given the clear evidence, these stations are able to secure substantial and increasing fees; they are more than capable of negotiating their channel position, as well.

Removing government's thumb from the scale will allow companies to negotiate more flexible packages and free consumers to secure broadcast channels over-the-air for free as intended and not have to pay for them as part of their cable subscription. This outdated requirement only applies to cable operators and not other MVPDs, and, given that cable represents only half of the market today, the must-buy rule imposes a significant and unjustified disadvantage on cable operators.

Thank you for inviting me today and I look forward to your questions.

[The prepared statement of Mr. Powell follows:]

PREPARED STATEMENT OF HON. MICHAEL K. POWELL, PRESIDENT AND CHIEF
EXECUTIVE OFFICER, NATIONAL CABLE & TELECOMMUNICATIONS ASSOCIATION

Good afternoon, Mr. Chairman and members of the Subcommittee. My name is Michael Powell and I am the President and Chief Executive Officer of the National Cable & Telecommunications Association. Thank you for inviting me today to offer our thoughts on "Reauthorization of the Satellite Television Extension and Localism Act."

Mr. Chairman, we support the Committee's effort to extend expiring provisions in the Communications Act and appreciate your consideration of other reforms to ensure the law protects and promotes the competitive video marketplace that is delivering consumers significant choice, innovative new ways to enjoy video content and a plethora of creative and diverse programming. A primary concern for Congress is the anticipated expiration of the current Communications Act provision that requires broadcasters and MVPDs to negotiate in good faith when conducting retransmission consent negotiations. By extending the "good faith" requirement for another five years, the Committee would ensure that this bilateral legal obligation remains part of the retransmission consent regime.

In addition to extending the "good faith" requirement, we believe a few additional reforms are appropriate, and in fact, are overdue given the competitive realities of today's video marketplace. As we noted in our written responses to the questions previously posed by Senators Rockefeller, Thune, Wicker, and Pryor, NCTA has identified three narrow, yet very important, reforms that would prune away outdated legal requirements, directly benefit consumers and promote a more level playing field among competing providers of multichannel video services.

First, NCTA supports repeal of the Federal Communications Commission ("FCC")'s "integration ban" rule, which today forces cable operators—and cable operators alone—to include a separate video decryption component (*e.g.,* a CableCARD) in their leased set-top boxes, adding extra cost, consuming extra energy, and providing no added benefit to cable customers with leased set-top boxes.

Second, we support codifying the FCC's effort to prohibit broadcasters that are not commonly owned from engaging in joint negotiations with cable operators and other MVPDs for the price, terms and conditions of their retransmission consent. Through a variety of formal and informal agreements, certain broadcasters have been increasing their leverage in the negotiations by banding together and acting as a single entity in the negotiations rather than acting appropriately as competitors. The Department of Justice and the FCC have raised significant concerns about these anticompetitive practices, and it is appropriate for Congress to address this issue as a complement to actions being taken at the FCC.

Third, we would similarly support efforts to amend the so-called "must buy" requirement, which currently affords stations that elect to negotiate retransmission consent with a duplicative, government-created windfall. Put simply, the right to negotiate retransmission consent already affords broadcast stations with the power to negotiate carriage terms, including price and channel position, on the cable system. Accordingly, the added legal obligation imposed on cable operators to carry such stations as part of a government-required basic tier is not only duplicative, but is also unfair given the lack of a similar legal obligation imposed on non-cable MVPDs. Indeed, the requirement that cable operators *alone* among all video programming distributors must offer a "must buy" basic tier already imposes a significant and unjustified competitive disadvantage on cable operators. The law should not heighten that disparity by supplementing the right of retransmission consent stations to negotiate terms of carriage with a legal obligation guaranteeing that such carriage occurs within the cable operator's basic tier of service.

As the Committee considers the course and speed of its legislative initiatives, we would urge members to include these issues as areas that are ripe for legislative reform.

Congress Should Extend The Mutual Obligation To Negotiate Retransmission Consent in Good Faith

NCTA supports the proposed five-year extension of the legal obligation to negotiate retransmission consent in good faith. Broadcast programming remains an important part of the cable service offering, and ensuring that negotiations for the carriage of broadcast programming on cable are conducted honestly, in a good faith attempt to reach a mutually beneficial carriage agreement, is essential. Continuing a duty of good faith works to constrain excessive demands for unreasonable terms and conditions and, when faithfully applied, limits the risk of blackouts or other actions that harm consumers. Accordingly, we support the extension of this requirement for five years, which helps to preserve consumer expectations and is consistent with the terms sought in prior efforts to extend expiring provisions.

The FCC's Integration Ban Imposes Needless Costs On Cable Customers And Is Not Needed To Promote Competition In Retail Video Device Availability

NCTA asks the Committee to consider including legislative language, present in bipartisan legislation (H.R. 3196) introduced by Congressmen Latta (R–OH) and Green (D–TX), that would repeal a technology mandate adopted by the FCC in 1998 that eliminated a low cost choice for consumers, wastes energy, slows innovation, violates principles of competitive neutrality, and is unnecessary to fulfill the stated statutory objective of promoting the competitive availability of retail navigation devices such as set-top boxes.

Congress intended as part of the 1996 Act to create the conditions for a *retail* market for set-top boxes and other navigation devices. The FCC was charged with making it possible for manufacturers to develop and sell devices that could be used, for example, with any cable provider anywhere in the country. Importantly, Congress did not impose any technical requirements on existing set-top boxes *leased* by cable operators to their own subscribers.

In carrying out Congress's 1996 directive to promote a new market where consumers could choose to buy set-top boxes and other navigation devices at retail rather than lease them from their provider, the FCC did two things. First, it required the cable industry—and only the cable industry—to develop a separate security device to unscramble cable signals, now known as the CableCARD, for use in set-top boxes and other navigation devices that could be sold at retail and used on any cable system. If a customer moved, he could return the CableCARD to his former cable provider, and get a new CableCARD from his new cable provider, which would unscramble *that* provider's signals. This "separate security" requirement fulfilled Congress's mandate of facilitating the creation of a *retail* market for set-top boxes and other navigation devices.

The FCC, however, took a second and unnecessary step, adopting the so-called "integration ban." It required cable operators to completely redesign their *own* leased set-top boxes to use CableCARDs, thereby prohibiting the integration of security (encryption) and navigation (channel-changing) functions in set-top boxes. This required operators to strip out security functions that had long been integrated in leased boxes. The idea behind this "integration ban" was that if operators had to rely on CableCARDs in their own boxes, they would have strong incentives to support CableCARDs in retail devices as well. Moreover, by eliminating a low cost leasing option, the FCC was attempting—through a little industrial engineering—to steer consumers to choose new third party options.

With the benefit of hindsight, we can now clearly see that while CableCARDs are a "fully realized solution" (to quote TiVo), the integration ban has not stimulated a consumer appetite for third-party devices. Today, more than 45 million CableCARD-enabled set-top devices have been deployed by cable operators to their customers, but a mere 600,000 CableCARDs have been requested by cable customers for use in third-party devices purchased at retail. Very few televisions contain CableCARD slots. This is not for lack of cable industry support of CableCARDs, but because manufacturers have found that consumers are not interested in paying the higher price for TVs with built in set-top technology.

Consumers that elect a cable operator's leased box, however, are paying a penalty in unnecessary expense and energy costs. Recent evidence filed with the FCC just last year by one large cable operator seeking a waiver of the ban indicated that "the cost of including a CableCARD and card interface in its current set-top boxes is in the $40 to $50 range." We estimate that the costs attributable to the integration ban exceed $1 billion for the cable industry. Additionally, based on EPA figures, cable subscribers collectively foot the bill for roughly 500 million kilowatt hours consumed by CableCARDs each year. By all measures, the costs of this misguided rule clearly outweigh its benefits.

Further evidence of the integration ban's incoherence is that these financial costs and energy burdens are borne only by cable subscribers and not video customers of satellite providers, like DirecTV and DISH, or of telco providers, like AT&T. Despite these providers being vigorous competitors, they have no CableCARD obligations, creating an unlevel playing field. At the time the rule was adopted, cable had a very large market share, and there may have been an arguable case for a rule exclusively applied to cable. Today, however, that share has shrunk from roughly 85 percent to just over 50 percent. DirecTV and DISH are the second and third largest providers of multichannel video programming, and AT&T is the fifth largest MVPD. The integration ban hampers cable's ability to compete fairly in this dynamic marketplace, and there is no substantive justification for this disparate regulatory treatment. Further, the goal of advancing a national market for third-party devices is illusory when the ban is applied to only half of the market.

It is important to note that even if the FCC-created integration ban is repealed, cable operators will still be required to provide CableCARDs or other separate security for devices purchased at retail. Third party set-top box makers, like TiVo, will still be able to build boxes that use CableCARDs, and cable operators will be required to support those devices. Beyond a cable operator's continued legal obligation, it will have a strong incentive to continue to support CableCARDs, given that 45 million CableCARD-enabled set-top boxes are in customer homes and that at least seven domestic cable operators are using TiVo as a primary leased set-top box. Repeal of the integration ban simply gives cable customers more choices and lower costs.

Repeal of the integration ban also will not interfere with opportunities for innovation in retail set-top boxes. CableCARD technology is limited to decrypting video programming so that customers can view the channels to which they have subscribed. It does not prevent manufacturers from pursuing new retail products and services now or in the future. The innovative TiVo Roamio DVR is today much more advanced than prior TiVo boxes, yet the CableCARD is the same.

The fact is that the navigation device goals of the 1996 Act are being achieved. As the FCC noted in its most recent Video Competition Report, "the CPE marketplace is more dynamic than it has ever been, offering consumers an unprecedented and growing list of choices to access video content." Cable operators have been key actors in facilitating these marketplace developments by making their services available on a broad and growing array of CE devices. Numerous cable operators are delivering cable services to iOS and Android tablets and smartphones, PCs and Macs, and game consoles and other video devices, and that trend is accelerating to meet consumer demand for these options. These devices that consumers want do not rely on CableCARDs. Today's competitive market is obviously providing plenty of incentives for cable operators to make their customers happy without needing cable to adopt the same technology solutions for their own set-top boxes.

Retail competition in navigation devices is a worthy goal, but it is now clear that this goal is best supported by embracing the innovations already occurring in today's retail marketplace and not by clinging to an outdated and costly FCC rule. The repeal of the integration ban will not change the path for innovation in the retail set-top box but will provide more opportunities for innovation in operator-supplied boxes, which will no longer have to be engineered around the CableCARD. We are pleased that the bill advanced last week by the House Committee on Energy and Commerce's Subcommittee on Communications and Technology includes a provision repealing the integration ban that enjoyed strong bipartisan support, and we respectfully suggest that any reauthorization bill advanced by this Committee should similarly remove this outdated and harmful rule.

Prohibiting Broadcast Stations From Coordinating Their Retransmission Consent Negotiations Unless Co-Owned Would Create A More Stable Carriage Environment For Consumers

It is important that any reform seek to promote balance in retransmission consent negotiations. Congress originally created the retransmission consent provisions in an attempt to achieve a competitive balance between the cable and broadcast industries and believed that the retransmission consent negotiation process would provide incentives for both parties to come to mutually beneficial arrangements. Given government's substantial involvement in what would otherwise be a free market negotiation, government has an even greater responsibility to police anticompetitive attempts to gain undue market power.

In recent years, certain broadcaster practices have disrupted that competitive balance. One of the more troubling practices is that broadcasters are using a variety of formal and informal agreements to coordinate the prices, terms, and conditions they agree to with MVPDs for their retransmission consent.

If multiple broadcast stations in a local market are not co-owned, then they should not be allowed to *act* as if they are co-owned in retransmission consent negotiations. The Department of Justice has voiced concerns about broadcast stations that are not commonly owned jointly coordinating their retransmission consent negotiations. DOJ argues that broadcasters must be required to exercise retransmission consent rights individually, because joint negotiations strengthen the broadcasters' negotiating positions against MVPDs, allowing the stations to obtain better deals, and because joint negotiations eliminate competitive rivalry between the stations. As a result, these joint negotiations result in higher prices and less choice for consumers.

FCC Chairman Wheeler recently recognized this point, noting that "joint negotiations have been documented to increase prices to cable systems," which "ultimately are borne by the consumer in the form of higher cable or Direct Broadcast Satellite fees." The Commission may soon act, justifiably, to eliminate these practices by making joint negotiations a *per se* violation of a broadcaster's obligation to negotiate in good faith when the broadcasters are not commonly owned and are among the top four stations in the local market, and a presumptive violation of that obligation for all other broadcasters in the local market.

As the Committee considers this issue, we would urge it to take actions that complement and extend FCC efforts. NCTA believes that non-commonly owned broadcasters should not be allowed to coordinate their retransmission consent negotiations in any way—whether through directly or indirectly exchanging or sharing information regarding the terms of existing retransmission consent agreements, the potential terms of future retransmission consent agreements, or the status of ongoing retransmission consent negotiations.

Retransmission Consent Broadcast Stations Should Not Be Automatically Included In Cable Operators' "Must Buy" Basic Tier.

Another area ripe for reform is the scope of the "must buy" obligations that apply under current law. In particular, NCTA believes that one warranted change would limit "must buy" basic tier requirements to broadcast stations electing must-carry status and certain other required channels, such as PEG channels required by the franchising authority to be carried on the basic tier. Retransmission consent stations should not have a government-mandated right to be included in that "must buy" tier.

Not only is a government-imposed "must buy" requirement for retransmission consent stations unwarranted, it is also selectively applied. Under current law, it is cable operators *alone* who are required to offer a "must buy" basic tier. No other MVPD or its customers is subject to a statutory "must buy" requirement. This requirement imposes a significant and unjustified competitive disadvantage on cable operators.

Eliminating the requirement that cable operators carry broadcast stations electing retransmission consent on the basic tier would not fully rectify this competitive imbalance, but it would promote greater competitive neutrality among video distributors. Retransmission consent stations would continue to negotiate with cable operators over channel placement and price, but having elected to privately negotiate carriage terms, would no longer enjoy the unwarranted additional benefit of a government-created requirement for mandatory carriage in the must-buy tier. Eliminating this requirement would also mean that consumers do not have to pay for such broadcast stations as a condition of receiving cable service.

NCTA appreciates your continued efforts to support a vibrant and innovative video marketplace. We look forward to working further with the Subcommittee on these important issues.

Thank you again for the opportunity to appear today.

Senator PRYOR. Senator Rockefeller.

STATEMENT OF HON. JOHN D. ROCKEFELLER IV, U.S. SENATOR FROM WEST VIRGINIA

Chairman ROCKEFELLER. Mr. Chairman, I apologize. Well, I thank you and apologize to everybody else for interrupting in this way but I have to go do some intelligence reading for a very important vote tomorrow. So I want to make a statement and I'm going to proceed to do that unless, of course, Senator McCaskill objects. In which case, I'll simply go to the back of the room and hide under a chair. Is it all right?

[Laughter.]

Senator McCASKILL. If you're good.

Chairman ROCKEFELLER. Good, thank you.

I want to thank Senator Pryor very much for convening today's Subcommittee hearing on the reauthorization of STELA. And I also want to applaud him. I was going to give a speech at the caucus but we never got called on. That if people would just listen to what we had in mind for cybersecurity, there never would have been this 170 million person data breach problem. It would have never happened. But people don't listen.

I also want to applaud him for his leadership of the communications subcommittee of which I'm very proud that he is the Chair and through work that he has done to help the Committee members understand the state of the communications marketplace, which is a very interesting phenomenon, and the pressing issues facing consumers in the companies that serve them.

Today, the Subcommittee considers, once again, the reauthorization of key statutes that promote competition in our video marketplace. Over the past 20 years, satellite pay-TV providers have extended pay-television service to consumers in rural areas, which did not have such service prior to that.

Across the country, they've offered consumers an alternative to their local cable provider. Today, DIRECTV and DISH Network have become the second and third largest national pay-TV providers. STELA and its predecessors, along with other necessary competitive protections from the 1992 Cable Act, who will ever forget those days, have been essential to satellite's growth.

Congress recognized early on that it must act to foster competition and enhance consumer choice in the video market. Now we are faced once again with the question of whether to reauthorize key elements of STELA. Let me be clear: I believe that we would do customers a disservice if we failed to reauthorize STELA.

Approximately 1.5 million satellite subscribers continue to rely on STELA for access to broadcast television. Hundreds of thousands of homes in West Virginia have subscribed to satellite television. And every pay-TV consumer benefits from the protection afforded by the law's requirement that broadcast, cable and satellite, negotiate in good faith. They're wonderful words. If only they came true.

The pending reauthorization also gives the Committee a chance to reassess whether the overall video marketplace operates to the benefit of consumers and competition. Since the last time we addressed STELA, this committee has held nearly six hearings. Well I guess we've held six hearings; not nearly. We've held six hearings exploring the video marketplace. The record from those hearings shows that several aspects of the present video market could be reformed. And as you know, I think it is long since time to explore what we can do to foster a more consumer-centric future for video, particularly through online video distribution.

There are some who believe that STELA is not the appropriate time to address these issues. They argue that such an examination is better left for some future day as part of the mythical rewrite of the Communications Act; which always seems to be right around the next corner. I know there is a pent-up desire among the Committee members to fully debate and address these issues, issues that directly affect all of our constituents.

I've been part of this committee for three decades now and participated in many debates over video policy. Although the final path for STELA reauthorization has not been determined, one of the things that I have learned from my tenure here is that committees should seize the opportunities that present themselves, not take a pass for another day. That future day may not come. Dealing with these issues will require the Committee to take a close look at today's video market, ask tough questions, and, ultimately, we may have to make hard choices that may upset incumbent interests. And so be it.

For me, the touchstone will always be whether the Committee's STELA reauthorization legislation advances the public interest. I think it's fair to say that there's a good chance that this will not be a clean process this year. I'm confident that this committee will be able to work in a bipartisan fashion to reauthorize STELA and I thank the witnesses for coming today and for putting up with my interruption.

I thank the Chair.

[The prepared statement of Chairman Rockefeller follows:]

PREPARED STATEMENT OF HON. JOHN D. ROCKEFELLER IV,
U.S. SENATOR FROM WEST VIRGINIA

I want to thank Senator Pryor for convening today's Subcommittee hearing on the reauthorization of the Satellite Television Extension and Localism Act, or STELA. I also want to applaud him for his leadership of the Communications Subcommittee and the thorough work he has done to help the Committee members understand the state of the communications marketplace, and the pressing issues facing consumers and the companies that serve them.

Today, the Subcommittee considers once again the reauthorization of key statutes that promote competition in our video marketplace. Over the past 20 years, satellite pay TV providers have extended pay television service to consumers in rural areas which did not have such service previously. Across the country, they have offered consumers an alternative to their local cable provider. Today, DirecTV and Dish Network have become the second and third largest national pay TV providers.

STELA and its predecessors, along with other necessary competitive protections from the 1992 Cable Act, have been essential to satellite's growth. Congress recognized early on that it must act to foster competition and enhance consumer choice in the video market. Now, we are faced once again with the question of whether to reauthorize key elements of STELA.

Let me be clear: I believe that we would do consumers a disservice if we failed to reauthorize STELA:

- Approximately 1.5 million satellite subscribers continue to rely on STELA for access to broadcast television;
- Hundreds of thousands of homes in West Virginia subscribe to satellite television; and
- Every pay TV consumer benefits from the protection afforded by the law's requirement that broadcast, cable, and satellite negotiate in good faith.

The pending reauthorization also gives the Committee a chance to reassess whether the overall video marketplace operates to the benefit of consumers and competition. Since the last time we addressed STELA, this Committee has held nearly half a dozen hearings exploring the video marketplace. The record from those hearings shows that several aspects of the present video market could be reformed. And as you know, I think it is long since time that to explore what we can do to foster a more consumer-centric future for video, particularly through online video distribution.

There are some who believe that STELA is not the appropriate time to address these issues. They argue that such an examination is better left for some future day, as part of a mythical rewrite of the Communications Act, which always seems to be right around the corner. I know there is a pent up desire among the Committee members to fully debate and address these issues—issues that directly affect all of our constituents.

I have been part of this Committee for three decades and participated in many debates over video policy. Although the final path for the STELA reauthorization has not been determined, one of the things that I have learned from my tenure is that the Committee should seize the opportunities that present themselves, not take a pass for another day. That future day may not come.

Dealing with these issues will require the Committee to take a close look at today's video market, ask tough questions, and ultimately we may have to make hard choices that may upset incumbent interests. For me, the touchstone will always be whether the Committee's STELA reauthorization legislation advances the public interest. I am confident that this Committee will be able to work in a bipartisan fashion to reauthorize STELA. And as we have with past STELA reauthorizations, we will work closely with Senator Leahy and the Judiciary Committee.

I thank the witnesses for coming today and welcome their thoughts on the STELA reauthorization.

Senator PRYOR. Thank you, Mr. Chairman.
Mr. Rogers.

STATEMENT OF THOMAS S. ROGERS, PRESIDENT AND CHIEF EXECUTIVE OFFICER, TiVo INC.

Mr. ROGERS. Thank you, Mr. Chairman.

My name is Tom Rogers; I am President and CEO of TiVo. In my career, I have been counsel to the House Telecommunications Subcommittee, your counterpart on the other side, in the 1980s. When I left Capitol Hill, I became the first President of NBC cable and had the privilege of founding CNBC. I have been CEO of TiVo for eight years. I drafted the Cable Act of 1984, which was key legislation that deregulated the cable industry. Also, this happened to be the first legislation that assured access to signals for satellite dish owners. I have worked tirelessly through my career to advance the interest of the cable industry and try to promote competition and consumer choice.

TiVo stands for innovation. I am particularly proud of Mr. Powell's statement when he was Chairman at the FCC calling TiVo "God's machine." It was one of the best quotes we have in support of our product.

Today, more than ever, I work to advance the competitive position of cable operators. Along these lines, given how this issue has been framed, I find it very odd that anyone would cast us as anti-cable on any issue, especially the CableCARD issue that the Committee has asked for comments on.

In addition to our retail consumer set-top business, which is well known, today we count as partners 14 of the top 20 cable operators in the United States. We not only provide consumers a choice at retail but we are dedicated to getting cable operators the best possible customer experience. And all of our cable partners recognize that we have given them a huge upgrade in terms of their future technology relative to the lackluster look and feel that most cable operators have been known for in their video service.

We spend more time, by a lot, serving the cable operators' future technology interests in this regard than others serving the cable industry, including NCTA. This is what we do. Our lifeblood is about driving the future technology for television viewers, including cable subscribers.

And while, with all due respect to Mr. Powell, and I do understand what the role of trade associations are, but the position that NCTA has taken on this CableCARD issue is not what's in the best interest for cable subscribers and it's not even what's in the best technological interest of cable operator members. The ability to port to cable operators what we do derives directly from the fact that there was a retail consumer business made possible by CableCARDs. Operators have benefited hugely from the retail business that we've created.

Now, having said that, we understand the cost burden of CableCARDs. We understand it well. We have our own issues with CableCARDs, not least of which is the problems consumers have had having them installed by cable operators who are not well trained on the installation. So we are here to represent three points of view.

Choice for consumers is good. In every other area, telephone, smartphone, laptop, name the device, consumers have the right to bring their own. The exception to that has been in the television set-top box arena, which is the one area where consumer choice and competition in that regard has not been provided as a means for consumers to have choice.

Two, we are extremely invested in the future technology for cable operators and we want to see cable operators succeed in terms of being the leaders in future television technology.

And third, we get the fact that there is a better approach than CableCARDs. In our view, there's one, and only one, way to do it and it's not the way that the House legislation has put forward. We need to get to a new standard that replaces CableCARDs; a downloadable security standard that doesn't rely on a physical card having to be inserted in a box. A new standard will save operators money, will assure competition and choice for consumers, and will continue to assure that our great innovations that we provide to the cable industry will continue to be easily ported to them.

One theme that's critical in underlying that approach is that we need common reliance, which has become the industry term for the security standard that operator boxes provide and that retail set-top boxes rely on. That's the linchpin for having a retail market.

Now, what the legislation on the House side tries to do is repeal the CableCARD standard before a new standard is in place, which in our minds will kill any ability for a new standard to emerge. What will happen is different operators will use different solutions which will kill any prospect for a national retail market. We need a standard; not a regulation. A standard. There's a smart way to do this. All policymakers ask that key cable companies and TiVo sit down and figure out that next generation standard that isn't a burden on cable that provides for choice and consumer competition. And, when that is in place, then the CableCARD regime should certainly go away.

Thank you, Mr. Chairman.

[The prepared statement of Mr. Rogers follows:]

PREPARED STATEMENT OF THOMAS S. ROGERS, PRESIDENT
AND CHIEF EXECUTIVE OFFICER, TIVO INC.

Good afternoon, Chairman Pryor, Ranking Member Wicker, and members of the Subcommittee. Thank you for the opportunity to participate in today's hearing. My name is Tom Rogers and I am the President and Chief Executive Officer for TiVo Inc. TiVo developed the first commercially available DVR and is the leading provider of competitive retail Set-Top Boxes with over 4 million subscribers worldwide, including approximately 1 million U.S. retail subscribers.

I appreciate the invitation to testify before you today to discuss whether the current law appropriately protects and promotes a video market that is responsive to consumer demands and expectations. Fundamentally, the Satellite Television Extension and Localism Act and the predecessor legislation, are about competition. The Act has given consumers choice in how they access multichannel programming. Competition and consumer choice should be the hallmark of any satellite reauthorization.

Extraneous provisions that actually undermine consumer choice and competition have no place in STELA reauthorization legislation. For this reason, TiVo opposes the legislation recently reported out of the House Communications and Technology Subcommittee which includes language that would undermine consumers' ability to purchase their own Set-Top Box to watch their cable channels. We urge this Committee to reject this anti-consumer provision.

There is a long established policy of allowing consumers to bring their own device that defines the features and experience they want to use with their network. History has shown time and again that when devices are untethered from the network and consumers have choice, innovation is unleashed. We need no better examples of this than the smart phone, the tablet, and the laptop. Consumers have device choice in most of the industries that meet their communications needs.

The one glaring exception is in the multichannel video sector. Ninety-nine percent of multichannel video provider customers use operator-supplied Set-Top Box equipment. While the cost of consumer electronics are consistently decreasing, the price charged to consumers to lease Set-Top Box equipment is consistently increasing. These are not the hallmarks of a competitive marketplace. More choice is needed and with more choice comes innovation and lower prices. A retail market allows for such choice, innovation, and ultimately lower pricing. TiVo has used the access to cable signals afforded by CableCARD to provide consumers with the option to purchase a product with features and functionality not provided by their cable operator. TiVo's latest Set-Top Box, called Roamio, is the only way for consumers to get their broadcast, cable, video-on-demand, and Internet-delivered content (such as Netflix, Amazon, Hulu Plus, YouTube) together in one user interface that enables the consumer to search across all of content offered through each of these services. TiVo's Roamio product has been heralded in the press as "the Holy Grail of Set-Top Boxes" (Wall Street Journal), "a big step up for cable TV subscribers" (TechHive), "the ultimate cable box,"[1] and "the best TV viewing experience that money can buy."[2]

TiVo stands for innovation. We are the innovators in multichannel video. TiVo not only was the first company to introduce the Digital Video Recorder, it was the first to make services like Amazon video rentals available on the television. TiVo also pioneered the ability to transfer cable television shows from a DVR to computers and mobile devices, and the integration of traditional television and over-the-top content into a seamless integrated user interface. No Set-Top Box (other than TiVo) is listed in CNET's top 20 most innovative consumer electronic products of the decade.[3] Nobody proclaims their love of a cable box. But they often do for TiVo.

Our retail products have pushed multichannel operators to improve their products and we continue to offer consumers features available only on our devices. I am not here to criticize cable, quite the contrary. TiVo is working with cable operators to offer their customers the best television experience possible. Many cable operators have told us how our retail business has hugely benefitted them because TiVo's retail devices have features and functionality that consumers want to pay for. TiVo's ability to provide choice and innovation to both retail consumers and operators depends on having access to the cable signals. Without access to the same channels as an operator-supplied box, a retail box cannot provide a real alternative to a consumer.

The provision slipped into STELA in the House bill would repeal the pro-competitive requirement that operators use the same security standard in their boxes as

---

[1] http://www.theverge.com/2013/8/20/4638390/tivo-roamio-pro-review
[2] http://venturebeat.com/2013/08/20/three-thumbs-up-for-the-new-tivo-roamio-dvrs/
[3] http://reviews.cnet.com/8301-18438_7-10413195-82.html

they make available for retail and jeopardize the ability of retail devices to access all cable programming channels. Common reliance on the same security standard is a principle that the Federal Communications Commission ("FCC") has repeatedly found is a necessary component for a retail market for Set-Top Boxes to emerge. Seeking its repeal is at odds with cable's generally pro-competitive policy approach. Cable originally provided competition to broadcast networks, then to data and telephone networks, and did not oppose the original STELA legislation that enabled satellite competition to cable.

In 1996 Congress, led by former Representative—now Senator—Markey had the wisdom to include in the landmark Telecommunications Act a provision to unlock the devices through which cable subscribers get their channels. The concept was simple—consumers should have the ability to purchase a navigation device or Set-Top Box at retail and not have to rely on renting a box from their cable provider. This provision was intended to do for the multichannel video device market what the Carterfone decision 45 years ago did for the telephone industry and what the Congress is currently doing for consumers with wireless devices. When consumers have choice, innovation flourishes because manufacturers have to compete on features and functionality to entice consumers to choose its products.

To implement this section, Section 629 of the 1996 Act, the FCC urged cable operators to reach agreement with the consumer electronics industry. Cable operators came forward with a standard CableCARD interface for national access by competitive entrant devices but did not promise to rely on this technology in their own devices. The FCC accepted this offer *provided* that cable operators (1) make CableCARDs available by July 1, 2000, and (2) rely on the CableCARD interface in their own newly fielded devices by January 1, 2005. The FCC determined that only by requiring "common reliance" by retail devices and operator-leased devices on the same security technology would retail devices receive the support necessary to attain the goals of Section 629.

The first CableCARD-reliant products—televisions with CableCARD slots—came to market in 2003–2004 but in the absence of common reliance received poor or nonexistent support from cable operators as documented in FCC and court decisions.[4] That lack of support finally led the FCC to implement common reliance on the same security technology (also known as the "integration ban") as of July 1, 2007. By this time, CableCARD televisions were disappearing from the market due to lack of cable operator support. But, the emergence of High Definition Television and the impending digital transition encouraged TiVo and others to begin selling HD CableCARD DVRs.

Because retail CableCARD devices were still being disadvantaged by cable operators,[5] the FCC in 2010 adopted rules to strengthen its CableCARD regulations to deal directly with certain cable operators' evasion of CableCARD requirements, by providing for consumer self-installation of CableCARDs, access to switched digital programming, and ending economic discrimination against competitive products.[6] While CableCARD success has been hobbled by a lack of support from certain cable providers and a refusal to allow retail devices to have access to two-way services like Video On Demand, CableCARD is a fully realized solution that provides consumers today with a choice of using a better alternative to an operator-supplied box.

The history of implementation of Section 629 shows that if Congress wants to promote choice and innovation, retail devices must have the same access to signals as operator-supplied devices. Allowing cable operators to treat the boxes they lease to subscribers differently than retail devices undermines retail choice and competition.

Even with CableCARD, certain cable operators have treated their own leased boxes differently and implemented switched digital video ("SDV") technology that denied retail devices direct access to numerous cable channels. SDV uses the two-way cable infrastructure for upstream signaling to request a channel be sent to the set-top box similar to video-on-demand. However, retail boxes have been prohibited from using the upstream capability of the cable network and are thus unable to receive SDV signals directly. Users of retail devices in SDV signals have thus been forced to use operator-provided equipment (so-called "tuning adapters") to enable

---

[4] *See, e.g., Charter Communications* v. *FCC*, 440 F.3d 31, 40–44 & n.10 (D.C. Cir. 2006); *In the Matter of Implementation of Section 304 of the Telecommunications Act of 1996, Commercial Availability of Navigation Devices*, CS Dkt. No. 97–80, Second Report and Order ¶ 39 & n.162 (Mar. 17, 2005)

[5] *See, e.g.*, Federal Communications Commission, Connecting America: The National Broadband Plan ("National Broadband Plan") § 4.2 at 52 ("[C]onsumers who buy retail set-top boxes can encounter more installation and support costs and hassles than those who lease set-top boxes from their cable operators.")

[6] *Implementation of Section 304 of the Telecommunications Act of 1996; Commercial Report and Order and Order on Reconsideration*, 25 FCC Rcd 14657 ¶ 5, 27 (2010).

their retail box to receive SDV signals, an approach antithetical to the goal of providing consumers with the choice to not use operator-provided equipment and still receive their cable channels.

That CableCARD is a flawed solution for retail is not new news. I am not here to defend the status quo. The issue confronting the Committee is how to *improve* the national standard that has allowed for retail competition, not how to repeal it.

There is an existing policy objective of ensuring that retail devices have access to cable signals so that competitive retail products can be created with innovative features and functionality. Without a uniform standard for accessing signals, a retail market cannot exist. TiVo would be happy to move to a new standard by which it can access cable signals. Legislation is not necessary to do that. All that is required is for a handful of companies to work cooperatively on a next generation standard under the supervision of the FCC that is non-burdensome and works for operators and retail devices. Repealing the existing uniform standard policy without putting a new standard in place will undermine competition, increase costs for consumers using retail devices, and eliminate any incentive for the industry to help develop a successor solution for retail devices. [7]

Congress needs to solve for the policy objective rather than undermining the existing policy in the name of lifting an industry burden that applies equally to retail devices and from which TiVo also wants to move on to a successor standard. The multichannel video industry is confronting its own IP transition. Now is the time to unleash innovation and give consumers the benefits of choice and competition in video devices like they have Internet, telephone and wireless devices.

The NCTA has been characterizing the repeal of the integration ban as a minor change and claiming that they still have to support retail CableCARD products.[8] Again, allowing operator-supplied boxes to use a different security standard than retail boxes results in a tilted playing field that undermines retail choice and competition. Moreover, the NCTA and some of its members are simultaneously taking the position at the FCC that there are no rules requiring them to provide or support CableCARDs to retail devices (and the FCC should not reinstate any rules unintentionally vacated by the DC Circuit Court of Appeals in a decision, *EchoStar* v. *FCC*, that did not even address the CableCARD rules.)[9]

This means that if the integration ban is eliminated, and if the FCC agrees with NCTA's position, there will be *no requirement* for cable operators use CableCARDs themselves and *no requirement* to supply CableCARDs to new retail devices. Indeed, *no requirement* for cable operators to even support existing retail CableCARD devices. Cable operators would be free to use new security technology but leave retail devices using legacy technology that they will have little incentive to support, keep

---

[7] The NCTA claims that CableCARD increases the cost of a set-top box by $56 citing an "estimate cited by the FCC" but this figure is based on data from 2008 or earlier—before common reliance and mass production lowered CableCARD costs. *See In the Matter of James Cable, LLC, RCN Corporation, WideOpenWest Finance, LLC Requests for Waiver of Section 76.1204(a)(1) of the Commission's Rules*, CSR–7216–Z, CSR–7113–Z, CSR–7139–Z, Memorandum Opinion and Order, 23 FCC Rcd. 10592 (2008) at **3, n.30. In the intervening 6 years, we believe that the unit cost of a CableCARD, when ordered in volume, has likely come down to about $10. The additional cost of the CableCARD interface for the set-top box, including additional software, has likely come down to about $2. The NCTA similarly estimates that the costs attributable to the integration ban exceed $1 billion without providing any support for this estimate. Whatever the cost of CableCARD, however, they pale in comparison to the over $7 billion per year that consumers pay to lease equipment from cable operators. This translates to approximately $50 billion in equipment lease revenue during the period of time that the NCTA claims to have incurred $1 billion in CableCARD costs. Whatever the cost, however, there is no justification for imposing the cost on retail devices but not on operator-supplied devices. These costs will surely rise again if operator-supplied devices are not using CableCARDs as there would no longer be mass production. Putting retail boxes at a cost and technology disadvantage certainly will not fulfill the goal of Section 629 of assuring a retail market.

[8] See Letter to The Honorable Greg Walden, Chairman, and The Honorable Anna Eshoo, Ranking Member, Subcommittee on Communications and Technology from James Assey, Executive Vice President, National Cable & Telecommunications Association dated September 18, 2013 at 2 ("repealing the integration ban will not affect the separate requirement for cable operators to make CableCARDs available to cable customers who buy a retail set top box from TiVo or others.")

[9] Opposition of Charter Communications, Inc. To Petition For Reconsideration, CSR–8740–Z, MB Docket No. 12–328 (June 3, 2013) at 3 n.6 (*"EchoStar* does not address downloadable security; what it changes is that CableCARD support is no longer required, and thus cable operators are free to rely solely on other compliant technologies . . ."); Comments of the National Cable & Telecommunications Association on TiVo Inc.'s Petition for Clarification or Waiver, CS Docket No. 97–80 (February 14, 2014); Comments of the National Cable & Telecommunications Association on TiVo Inc.'s Petition for Rulemaking, CS Docket No. 97–80, PP Docket No. 00–67 (September 16, 2013).

current with new technology developments, or control costs. Would anyone reasonably expect any consumer to purchase a retail set top box for the express purpose of replacing their cable-supplied Set-Top Box if there was no assurance that their cable operator would actually support that retail box? Retail devices have to be treated the same, in terms of access to programming and support, as operator-supplied devices for consumers to have a real choice and for the effects of competition to take hold.

In support of its position that no current rules and no next generation standard are needed to guarantee that retail devices have access to cable signals, the NCTA has tried to portray cable apps on Xbox or Roku as evidence of the emergence of a retail set top box market. While there has been some experimentation with apps on third party devices in the last couple of years, these experiments only serve to confirm that a successor security standard is essential. None of these apps *guarantee* that a consumer can purchase a retail device to (a) receive *all* of the cable programming they are paying for; (b) record that programming for later viewing; (c) incorporate Internet-delivered content; (d) frame the experience in a user interface better and more innovative than the lowest-common denominator approach supplied by their cable provider; and (e) work with more than one provider.[10] CableCARD does this for scheduled programming but it is clear that core MVPD services are moving on to IP technologies instead. Real device competition requires a successor solution in which consumers can have confidence that any retail devices they purchase for the purpose of receiving the cable programming to which they subscribe will be supported and will deliver their cable programming channels.

The removal of the AT&T U-verse app on X-Box last December confirms that apps provide no such assurance to consumers. AT&T U-verse had advertised its app on X-Box as an inducement for customers to sign-up for its service.[11] Then it abruptly announced that it would terminate support for its app on the Xbox 360 service.[12] The point is, these apps and other solutions come and go, and are not a reliable alternative to what is available on a competitive Set-Top Box where consumers are *guaranteed* access to all of their cable programming.

The video market is at a critical juncture with video about to undergo an IP transition. Now is the time to seize the opportunity to foster a next generation standard for accessing television signals. Ensuring that consumers have retail choices from unaffiliated Set-Top Box manufacturers, and that such retail devices are interoperable on networks nationwide, remains an essential, pro-consumer policy today. Indeed, the principle of requiring standards to enable competition in the market for communications equipment—leading in turn to consumer benefits in the form of greater innovation, lower prices, and higher quality—is one of the most settled and successful principles in telecommunications policy, and has been extremely successful in the wireline and wireless broadband markets.

This Committee can play a strong role on this important pro-competition and consumer choice issue by supporting a process that puts in place a more efficient market solution worked out between the industries. I respectfully urge you to support innovation and consumer choice and resist including any provisions in the STELA reauthorization bill that would undermine video device competition.

Senator PRYOR. Thank you.
Mr. Wood.

STATEMENT OF MATTHEW F. WOOD, POLICY DIRECTOR, FREE PRESS AND THE FREE PRESS ACTION FUND

Mr. WOOD. Chairman Pryor, Ranking Member Wicker, and Chairman Rockefeller, and members of the Subcommittee, thank you for the chance to testify today.

---

[10] Imagine buying an iPhone and then learning if you move to another community it no longer works because your local service provider won't support it. It's the same with these app experiments. They don't work across operators. Why would someone buy a Samsung TV that works today with Charter in Los Angeles knowing that if they move to Atlanta Cox won't support it? Retail choice requires national portability. CableCARD does this today and any successor standard must likewise be nationally portable.

[11] *http://www.prnewswire.com/news-releases/att-extends-tv-watching-to-more-devices-with-launch-of-u-verse-tv-on-xbox-360-104699739.html*

[12] *http://www.multichannel.com/distribution/att-u-verse-tv-drop-support-xbox-360-december-31/146904*

My name is Matt Wood and I'm the Policy Director for Free Press which is a nonpartisan, nationwide organization with more than 700,000 members. I'm glad to talk about STELA and will answer your questions about whether present law does enough to protect and promote a video marketplace that is responsive to consumer demands and expectations. The short answer is that Congress can and must do more to make sure that this market is functioning and free.

Television and broadband deliver video and other content that inform our democracy, shape our culture, and power our economy. No single speaker in our media system and no distributor in the middle of that system should have the power to dictate our discourse or control our programming. Competition in the marketplace of ideas requires competition among the channels and platforms that carry those ideas. And, as FCC Chairman Wheeler has said, "Competition does not always flourish by itself. It must be supported and protected."

Some companies and lobbyists call for reform or a total repeal of video rules. But don't be fooled. What they often want is changes that benefit their own business and hamper competitors. They'll suggest Congress should get rid of all safeguards. But the truth is that many laws on the books today actually promote competition and consumer choice that simply would not exist without them. We need laws built on bedrock principles of increasing choice, expanding access, preserving competition, and preventing discrimination.

Laws like STELA make more content available. STELA itself gives options to people that can't receive a local broadcast signal over the air. Congress should keep that option in place. Chairman Pryor, himself, and Mr. Palkovic noted that 1.5 million homes rely on distant signals for broadcast content and there's no reason to take that away or to narrow eligibility for them even more.

A better approach for improving access to local broadcasts would be to make sure satellite customers can get TV stations from their home state. Many of your constituents can't do that today, because Nielsen defines TV markets without regard for state lines. That's a problem because broadcast TV remains a primary source for news about our government and our communities. The FCC already has power to modify Nielsen markets and extending that power here would give the FCC a chance to make the call based on the facts of the individual circumstance.

Another expiring STELA provision is Section 325's requirement to negotiate retransmission consent in good faith. Congress should extend these protections, too, and could explain more about what the good faith standard requires or direct the FCC to do that. That's what the FCC did just yesterday; rightly deciding that joint negotiations by supposedly independent broadcasters don't meet that good faith standard.

Cable operators have seen increases up to 161 percent in the fees they pay when stations use these tactics. The FCC's action could control these skyrocketing costs that always come back to consumers. Congress also should clarify the FCC's authority to order carriage during retransmission disputes so that blackouts are not a bargaining chip.

Congress rolled back many Cable Act protections in 1996 and it now relies on competition to discipline those rates. But rates keep going up nearly three times the rate of inflation. That's because the method of gauging competition is not effective. Prices in markets that the Act calls "competitive" are actually 3 percent higher.

There's plenty of blame to go around for these failures. Too often pay-TV companies, broadcasters, and programmers divide the spoils from consumers that have no real choice in the market for bundled TV and broadband services. Cable operator revenues go up even as they lose video customers. Broadcast and cable channel revenues go up even as their ratings go down. But a lot of people have decided either they can't or they won't absorb these increases anymore. They're cutting the cord completely on pay-TV or relying more on online options.

Senator Rockefeller's Consumer Choice in Online Video Act would help online providers compete. It would guard against pay-TV attempts to deny content, degrade online choices or prop up their own video business by using their market power over broadband services.

The Television Consumer Freedom Act, sponsored by Senators McCain, Blumenthal, and Whitehouse, would lower prices by giving customers a real choice about what they buy. Letting people know what they're paying for each channel and letting them decide whether to pay it is common. It also would reduce blackouts by testing channel prices in a real market rather than tying up popular content in take-it-or-leave-it bundles.

Thank you very much and I look forward to your questions.

[The prepared statement of Mr. Wood follows:]

PREPARED STATEMENT OF MATTHEW F. WOOD, POLICY DIRECTOR, FREE PRESS AND THE FREE PRESS ACTION FUND

Introduction

Chairman Pryor, Ranking Member Wicker, and members of the Subcommittee, thank you for inviting me to testify on the Satellite Television Extension and Localism Act (STELA).

My name is Matt Wood, and I am the Policy Director for Free Press and the Free Press Action Fund. Free Press is a nationwide, nonpartisan and nonprofit organization with more than 700,000 members. We promote public interest media and technology policies, working to strengthen democracy by strengthening the tools we use for free expression and economic activity. We advocate for diverse media viewpoints and quality journalism. And we focus especially on promoting open, universal and affordable communications platforms for all.

In this testimony, I will comment first on the need to extend current laws that serve those same diversity and competition goals, including STELA and related provisions. Second, I will offer answers to the Committee's questions about whether present law does enough to protect and promote a video market responsive to consumer demands and expectations. Specifically, I will describe failures that permeate the industry, and address legislative proposals (in addition to STELA) that would allow consumers to enjoy more choices and more affordable services.

Some industry stakeholders today call for total "reform" of video marketplace rules—or, to describe their calls more accurately, for self-interested changes to benefit themselves and hamper their competitors. Their arguments suggest that a free market could exist for multichannel video programming distributor (MVPD) services or online video in the absence of any safeguards. But the truth is that many current measures actually promote competition and consumer choice that simply would not exist otherwise. Deleting some provisions and allowing others to expire (in the absence of a comprehensive, consumer-focused overhaul) would be especially harmful. So would ignoring the market power of established players.

Whether a particular statute or rule provision is necessary today is not an automatic binary choice, where public oversight is always bad and removing it is always good. The determination depends instead on the nature and the effect of the provision in question. Some rules actually work to limit the scope of copyright and contractual exclusivity provisions. So, like STELA, they make available certain types of content that it would be difficult or impossible to obtain in the absence of such rules.

Other existing provisions, like the good faith negotiation obligations in the retransmission consent context, are necessary to prevent anticompetitive behavior by incumbent providers and distributors. These provisions could be clarified, strengthened, or supplemented by new laws, such as the Consumer Choice in Online Video Act (CCOVA) (S.1680), sponsored by Senator Rockefeller; the Television Consumer Freedom Act of 2013 (TCFA) (S.912), sponsored by Senators McCain, Blumenthal and Whitehouse; and the Video CHOICE Act of 2013 (H.R. 3719), sponsored by Representatives Eshoo and Lofgren.

The Free Press Action Fund supports these bills because they would increase consumer choice among the offerings already on the market today. The CCOVA also would prevent harmful conduct leveled against new entrants in the video market by incumbent MVPDs that also offer broadband and, in some cases, control vertically integrated content companies as well.

Preserving and Extending Satellite Viewing Options

STELA and its predecessors, starting in 1988 with the Satellite Home Viewer Act (SHVA), were designed to address a technical gap and remedy the resulting limitation on viewer choice. SHVA and other STELA forerunners were intended to ensure that viewers who are unable to receive a local "over-the-air" broadcast signal could still have access to broadcast programming through their satellite television subscription.

Congress should continue to offer this assurance to such individuals, and should reauthorize STELA to provide continued satellite viewing options for unserved households. Prior reauthorizations of the satellite home viewing laws have narrowed the definition of "unserved households" and their eligibility for distant signals. Those bills have reduced opportunities for distant signal importation in favor of local-into-local carriage for in-market broadcast TV stations affiliated with the same network as the distant station.[1]

Free Press Action Fund takes no position on whether further legislative or regulatory action may be needed to implement these changes. We note, however, that direct broadcast satellite providers have testified that as many as 1.5 million homes still rely importation of distant signals for their broadcast content.[2] There is no reason to reduce these viewers' options by taking away signals they receive today.

STELA and other satellite laws should preserve and increase viewers' choices, not reduce them. Yet it remains the case today that any of many of your constituents are unable to watch in-state broadcast TV programming with their satellite subscription. That is because Nielsen draws its Designated Market Area (DMA) television market boundaries, on which the FCC relies, without regard for state lines. Certain counties are thus "orphaned" from the television stations located in the same state in which those themselves counties are located. This means that residents of a Nebraska county, for example, may be able to receive via satellite *only* television signals that originate in Iowa or Colorado; or that residents of a Wisconsin county may be eligible to receive only Minnesota broadcast television station signals.

This poses a problem because broadcast TV is a primary means by which residents get news and other information that is culturally relevant to their communities. Broadcasting also provides a medium through which elected officials communicate with their constituents, and through which those individuals can gather information about their representatives at the statehouse and in Congress too.

Under Section 614(h) of the Communications Act, 47 U.S.C. § 534(h), the Federal Communications Commission has the power to modify DMA boundaries for purposes of determining broadcast TV carriage rights on cable systems. The FCC's market modification processes under Section 614(h) would serve as a good precedent for addressing the issue of potentially misaligned boundaries that prevent residents from receiving any in-state broadcast signals either over-the-air or through their satellite provider. Use of the FCC's market modification procedures would not necessarily re-

---

[1] *See* 17 U.S.C. § 119(a)(3).

[2] *See, e.g.,* Testimony of Alison A. Minea, Director and Senior Counsel of Regulatory Affairs, DISH Network LLC, on "Reauthorization of the Satellite Television Extension and Localism Act," Hearing Before the United States Senate Committee on the Judiciary, at 3 (Mar. 26, 2014).

sult in changes to television market boundaries, or in the deletion of signals originating in the same DMA as the orphan county. This process would simply give the Commission a chance to make the determination based on the facts, and perhaps to "determine that particular communities are part of more than one television market."[3]

Keeping the Faith for Retransmission Consent Negotiations

Another expiring provision in STELA is the obligation under Section 325(b)(3)(C) of the Communications Act for broadcast television stations and MVPDs to negotiate retransmission consent agreements "in good faith." The Satellite Home Viewer Improvement Act (SHVIA) enacted in 1999, and the Satellite Home Viewer Extension and Reauthorization Act of 2004 (SHVERA), added these good faith negotiating requirements to the Communications Act—first for broadcasters, and then with a reciprocal good faith obligation for MVPDs as well.

Congress should extend these protections. It also could adopt additional specifications explaining what the good faith standard requires, or direct the FCC to provide such additional specifications in Section 76.65 of the Commission's rules. For instance, some have suggested that a broadcaster blocking access to its online content during a retransmission dispute—specifically aimed at broadband customers of an MVPD with whom the broadcaster's retransmission deal has expired—should be considered a bad faith negotiating tactic.[4]

Congress also should clarify the FCC's authority to order interim carriage of a television signal during the pendency of such retransmission consent disputes. Free Press supports the availability of a "standstill" period to ensure continued carriage when negotiations reach an impasse, so that viewers are not subjected to loss of service as a negotiating tactic.[5] Clarifying the FCC's authority to require carriage during the pendency of any such dispute would help hold viewers harmless and prevent them from bearing the brunt of such breakdowns in negotiations.

The brinksmanship and more frequent blackouts that go along with retransmission consent renewals deprive viewers of content they have already paid to watch. A better remedy than allowing importation of distant signals when a blackout begins, requiring refunds to MVPD subscribers after it is over, or creating a counter-productive "parity" to let MVPDs *delete* broadcast signals during ratings periods, would be to prevent loss of service in the first place.

Different parties have offered up persuasive if not definitive arguments about the FCC's *existing* authority to require interim carriage.[6] Clarifying the agency's authority (as Rep. Eshoo's Video CHOICE Act proposes) would remove any doubt about the FCC's ability to hold consumers harmless during a retransmission consent dispute. Such measures would preserve choice and rein in costs, but without scrapping retransmission consent compensation to broadcasters and content creators for use of their materials by the MVPDs who sell these signals to their own customers.[7]

Of course, to acknowledge that retransmission consent fees remain valid in principle is not to deny for a second that these fees are spiraling out of control. There are actions that the FCC has already undertaken to check these skyrocketing prices, and there are additional steps that Congress should take as well. These negotiations are not just a business disputes with no ramifications for consumers: the increased fees that MVPDs pay in such circumstances invariably are passed through to cable and satellite subscribers.

For instance, retransmission consent negotiations conducted jointly by broadcast TV stations allegedly under separate control—but in reality coordinating all of their operations—are one driver for this rising price of retransmitted broadcast signals. American Cable Association members have shown the increase in retransmission consent fees paid when stations employ these joint negotiating mechanisms. These small cable operators documented four instances in which the average impacts of

[3] 47 U.S.C. § 534(h)(1)(C)(i).

[4] *See, e.g.,* Harold Feld, Public Knowledge, "Escaping the Black Hole of Television Blackouts" (Aug. 6, 2013), *http://www.publicknowledge.org/news-blog/blogs/escaping-black-hole-television-blackouts.*

[5] *See, e.g.,* Comments of Free Press, Parents Television Council, and Consumers Union, MB Docket No. 10–71, *Petition for Rulemaking to Address the Federal Communications Commission's Rules Governing Retransmission Consent,* at 6–7 (filed May 18, 2010).

[6] *See, e.g.,* Letter from Public Knowledge, OTI, and the Benton Foundation, MB Docket No. 10–71, at 5–7 (filed Jan. 4, 2011); Letter from Public Knowledge, DISH, New America Foundation, DIRECTV, Charter Communications, American Cable Association and Time Warner Cable, MB Docket No. 10–71, at 1–4 (filed Dec. 11, 2013).

[7] *See, e.g.,* Testimony of Ellen Stutzman, Director, Research and Public Policy, Writers Guild of America, West, Inc., on "Reauthorization of the Satellite Television Extension and Localism Act," Hearing Before the United States Senate Committee on the Judiciary, at 3 (Mar. 26, 2014).

joint negotiations on their own retransmission consent costs were increases ranging from 21.6 percent to 161 percent.[8] MVPDs also have found more than 40 instances, representing more than 20 percent of all TV markets, in which a single broadcaster negotiates retransmission consent for more than one "big four" network affiliate—a number that will only grow in light of the continued pace of broadcast transactions.[9]

Free Press does not believe that congressional action is necessary at this time to prevent such joint negotiating tactics, so long as the FCC continues its progress towards renewed enforcement of the local television multiple ownership limits in Section 73.3555 of the Commission's rules. The FCC can prevent such coordination among alleged competitors by ensuring that separate broadcast licenses really do remain under separate control. That would prove a more effective remedy than a standalone ban on joint negotiations, while also working to promote competition, localism and diversity in other ways in local media markets.

Yet, breakdowns in retransmission consent negotiations do not exist in a vacuum, and the excesses and failures of the current video market would not disappear even if Congress and the FCC implemented all of the measures outlined above. Better faith bargaining, interim carriage requirements, and an end to joint retransmission consent negotiations would improve outcomes, but these steps would not by themselves allow consumers more freedom to choose their own video content—either on traditional MVPD platforms or from "over-the-top" alternatives.

That is why further congressional action *is* necessary, whether taken in conjunction with this reauthorization or not. Congress must address the real culprit for rising retransmission fees and myriad other failures in the video marketplace: the traditional cable business model, which too often centers around how to divide the spoils from captive customers rather than how to improve consumers' choices and lower their prices in the first place. These problems are not confined to the "traditional" video marketplace either, and they are now spilling over into online video and into our Nation's broadband communications market as well.

Additional Steps for Fixing America's Broken Video Market

America's video market is broken. Since 1996, when Congress relaxed the protections adopted in the Cable Television Consumer Protection and Competition Act of 1992, cable prices have risen steadily at nearly three times the rate of inflation. And this trend is only getting worse. Since the 2008 recession, the average annual rate of inflation has been 1.4 percent, but the price of expanded basic cable service has increased by an annual average of 5 percent. Plus, these figures do not include mandatory equipment rental costs, which continue to skyrocket too.

In fact, as Free Press has documented, the "effective competition" standard in Section 623 of the Communications Act, 47 U.S.C. § 543(*l*), has not succeeded in disciplining cable prices. Congress should modify that standard to make the FCC determine accurately whether effective competition really exists, rather than finding the mere presence of MVPDs other than incumbent cable to be "effective" even where cable's market share remains as high as 85 percent. This test simply does not measure whether competition actually occurs in such highly concentrated markets. That's the main reason that the FCC's own statistics show prices in markets deemed subject to effective competition under this test are 3 percent *higher*.[10]

While no one industry segment is responsible for all of these out-of-control price increases, there is plenty of blame to go around. Broadcast and cable channel owners such as Disney, Fox and Viacom, and multichannel video distributors like Comcast and Time Warner Cable, are the two factions of what Free Press has described as a comfortable cabal[11] that earns monopoly profits from consumers who are deprived of any real choice in the pay-TV market.

The recent recession took a brutal toll on many businesses. However, the cable, satellite and telco TV multichannel distributors kept making money. From 2007 to

---

[8]*See, e.g., Ex Parte* Comments of SuddenLink Communications, CSR Nos. 8233–C, 8234–M, at 5–6 (filed Dec. 14, 2009) (21.6 percent increase); USA Companies Letter to Ms. Marlene Dortch, Secretary, Federal Communications Commission, MB Docket No. 10–71 (filed May 28, 2010) (133 percent increase); Cable America Letter to Ms. Marlene Dortch, Secretary, Federal Communications Commission, MB Docket No. 10–71 (filed May 28, 2010) (161 percent increase); Pioneer Long Distance Letter to Ms. Marlene Dortch, Secretary, Federal Communications Commission, MB Docket No. 10–71 (filed June 4, 2010) (30 percent increase).

[9]*See, e.g.,* Notice of *Ex Parte* Communication of American Cable Association, MB Docket Nos. 10–71, 09–182, at 2 (filed June 24, 2013).

[10]*See* S. Derek Turner, Free Press, "Combatting the Cable Cabal: How to Fix America's Broken Video Market" (May 2013), *http://www.freepress.net/sites/default/files/resources/Combating_The_Cable_Cabal_0.pdf.*

[11]*See id.*

2011, the multichannel distributors collectively increased the price of expanded basic cable service by 22 percent. These rate hikes and other fee increases helped the industry boost its video-service revenues by 27 percent, an impressive performance considering that during this same period there was almost no growth in the total number of pay-TV subscribers.[12] Indeed, the traditional wired cable providers' total video revenues grew by 11 percent during this timeframe, even though these companies lost 11 percent of their subscribers.[13]

But these distributors are just that: distributors of (most often) someone else's programming. As the owners of that programming raise their fees, distributors either have to pass those higher costs along to their subscribers or accept lower profits on video. For many years, the distributors simply passed along all of these increased programming costs. As impressive as the multichannel video distributors' fiscal performance was through the recent economic downturn, it pales in comparison to the revenue growth experienced by cable programmers. From 2007 to 2011, total cable programmer revenues rose at a compound annual growth rate of 8 percent, a result analysts characterized as particularly impressive given the recession.[14]

Cable channels are not the only ones profiting from increased fees, as broadcasters also make extensive use of their retransmission consent rights today. Payments from multichannel video distributors to local broadcasters reach record levels every fiscal quarter, in some cases despite declining ratings. As one broadcast executive bragged to analysts: "[T]he reality of retransmission is it enables the broadcast business to be a healthy business. . . . [W]e have had a very disappointing year ratings-wise but our broadcast business is up [in] profitability."[15] Retransmission consent fees have risen across the board and become a larger and larger percentage of broadcasters' revenues. The industry saw retransmission revenues increase more than 10-fold in six years, from $215 million in 2006 to $2.4 billion in 2012.[16] They jumped to $3.3 billion in 2013, and current projections predict them more than doubling again to $7.6 billion in just five more years.[17]

While they often find themselves at odds over rates today, programmers and distributors still might work together to prevent consumers from truly "cutting the cord" for pay-TV services, or to keep customers from paying only for the programming those consumers want to watch. Many programmers leverage their ownership of high-demand channels (such as ESPN or HBO) and force MVPDs to purchase the less-desired channels controlled by these same programmers. Distributors long accepted this practices of wholesale bundling as acceptable or even beneficial for them as well, because they could pass the whole bundle on to customers. So MVPDs could grow their own revenues and create an illusion of value with ever-expanding channel lineups.

Recently, as programming fees continued to balloon, many consumers decided that either they couldn't or they wouldn't absorb the rate increases—leading to the decline in MVPD video subscribers documented above. As a result, MVPDs have been forced to absorb at least a portion of these increased programming costs. But cable companies are using their captive broadband customers to help shoulder the burden. Because the wired providers bundle video service with broadband, they are able to spread the programming-cost increases across each service in the bundle—maintaining healthy overall margins even as their video margins decline.

Lawmakers, including those on this Committee, have introduced or co-sponsored legislative solutions in the last year to these twin problems: limited choice in the TV channels that MVPD customers must buy, whether or not they watch them; and limited choice in the online alternatives that consumers have, both for watching broadcast and cable programming online and for utilizing alternative video sources. Free Press Action Fund has supported three such bills aimed at fixing these problems during the current Congress: Senator Rockefeller's CCOVA; the TCFA put forward by Senators McCain, Blumenthal and Whitehouse; and the Video CHOICE Act sponsored by Representatives Eshoo and Lofgren.

Increasing Consumer Choice on Pay-TV Platforms

The TCFA and the Video CHOICE Act address many of the same problems. The bipartisan TCFA in particular could shake up the industry and give consumers a real measure of control over the price they pay for the cable and broadcast channels

[12] *See id.* at 12.
[13] *See id.* at 2.
[14] *See id.* at 2.
[15] *Id.* at 19–20 (quoting News Corp. Q2 2013 Earnings Call, Feb. 6, 2013).
[16] *See id.* at 20.
[17] *See* "Retrans Rev Projected To Hit $7.6B By 2019," *TVNewsCheck,* Nov. 22, 2013, *http://www.tvnewscheck.com/article/72202/retrans-rev-projected-to-hit-76b-by-2019.*

made available to them. That bill virtually ensures that consumers would be offered an "à la carte" option alongside bundled-channel packages, allowing viewers to take and pay for only the channels they actually want to watch. This would save consumers money in the short run and, in the long run, help create a more competitive television market both online and on traditional MVPD platforms.

The Video CHOICE Act introduced by Reps. Eshoo and Lofgren seeks to prevent retransmission consent-driven blackouts by (1) enabling consumers to purchase cable service without subscribing to retransmitted broadcast stations and (2) prohibiting programmers from directly or indirectly condition retransmission consent on the carriage of additional, affiliated cable channels. (For example, prohibiting CBS from requiring carriage of Showtime to get the CBS signal.) The TCFA would go even further by providing incentives for retail à la carte for *all* pay-TV channels, including broadcast and cable programming alike.

Passage of these bills would promote competition between traditional MVPD services and online video alternatives, and increase market transparency and consumer agency in the purchase of traditional MVPD programming. If Congress does not pass such measures, large programmers will continue to tie less popular channels to their marquee content—crowding out capacity and opportunities for independent channels while making consumers foot the bill for an entire bundle of channels they don't want. Our research shows that the chief beneficiaries of forced bundling are not diverse programmers serving underserved communities, but sports and entertainment channels owned by Fox, Viacom, Comcast, Disney and the major sports leagues.[18]

In the absence of legislative action, retransmission consent and cable licensing fees will stay high because they are undisciplined by any real measure of demand. It's no surprise to see prices increase when the viewers ultimately purchasing this content have little to no knowledge of the price they pay for each channel, let alone the power to decide whether or not they purchase them. Such hidden prices are perhaps the most tangible sign of a failed market. Distributors sell inflexible, more-than-you-can-eat programming bundles full of channels that no one watches. This model completely obscures actual demand, making consumers appear to be far less price sensitive than they actually are for any given channel or group of channels.

Senator Rockefeller's CCOVA offers alternatives to the retransmission consent structure as well, by expressly authorizing antenna rental services (such as Aereo) and resolving doubts and ongoing litigation about the legitimacy of such services. But Senator Rockefeller's bill offers even more promise for video consumers because it expands not only the choices that viewers have with their current pay-TV subscriptions, but protects online content and distribution alternatives as well.

Increasing Video Options Online

The CCOVA would help online video content companies and distributors compete with traditional pay-TV channels and MVPDs. In no uncertain terms, it would prevent broadband Internet service providers from trying to squelch alternatives to their legacy video services. The bill would give online video providers more rights to negotiate access to popular content. It would keep broadband providers from degrading online video services that compete with traditional cable TV offerings. And it would clarify broadband billing to guard against discriminatory pricing, and to let consumers know what they are paying for.

The Free Press Action Fund endorsed the CCOVA because the bill would extend nondiscrimination and program access-style protections to online video providers, and more generally guard against anticompetitive practices (such as the use of data caps, forced bundling and exclusivity) when such practices are aimed at diminishing competition from online video sources. The bill notes the substantial First Amendment interest in "promoting a diversity of views" and would prohibit Internet Service Providers affiliated with MVPDs from favoring their own offerings.

These tactics harm not only the video market, including new entrants, innovators, and consumers in that market. They also harm broadband as well, as some MVPDs use their broadband service—a product subject to very little competition in a market with insurmountable entry barriers—to cross-subsidize their video business. Some large distributors like Comcast actually use predatory pricing (*e.g.,* selling a video-data bundle for less than the price of stand-alone data service) to discourage competition from new video providers. And some distributors like Comcast and AT&T use data caps and veiled threats against Internet openness to thwart competition from over-the-top competitors.

---

[18] *See* Turner, "Combatting the Cable Cabal," at 22–27.

Conclusion

Congress should reauthorize STELA, in the process preserving and expanding choices available to satellite viewers, while extending and strengthening good faith negotiating rules for retransmission consent. Yet the ultimate answer to preventing blackouts, and loss of service for consumers who already pay too much for video in the first place, is to empower those consumers with the ability to make decisions for themselves. Whether it takes up such reforms in this reauthorization process or not, Congress should allow the FCC to continue implementing its own retransmission consent and local ownership reforms. Congress also should enact new legislation to preserve and promote video choice both online and on traditional pay-TV platforms.

Senator PRYOR. Thank you.

And we've been joined by Senator Thune. And he has said that he does not want to ask questions. And as a reminder to the Committee, we will—I mean—I'm sorry. He said he didn't want to make a statement.

And as a reminder to the Committee, we will allow everyone to submit their full statements for the record, including the panel.

Let me jump in, if I may. Mr. Palkovic, let me ask you a pretty straightforward question, or at least it seems straightforward to me. And that is, the STELA and its predecessors have generally included a 5-year sunset and as Congress looks at this reauthorization, is 5 years the right amount of time? And also, is it 5 years for everything in the reauthorization or should there be, sort of, a staggered set? And if so, why?

Mr. PALKOVIC. Well, actually, I think that we would strongly support as long a term as you would consider. As it sits today, we are definitely not on a level playing field with cable which is our number one competitor who has a statutory license that does not sunset.

You know, permanent reauthorization would be what we would want. And then, as marketplace changes dictate, we would come back to the Committee with issues like blackout issues as appropriate. Right now, we have the uncertainty of coming back every 5 years and, because of that, we think that's the opportune time to not just extend it but to consider what's taken place in the last 5 years that would require Congress to change.

So longer is better for us.

Senator PRYOR. OK.

And I was going to ask you if you, I know that you—also, obviously, previously with the chairmanship of the FCC, you are in a unique position here, we all know that the video marketplace has changed a whole lot in the last years and continues to change. What do you think, what do you foresee the video marketplace to look like over the next four or 5 years?

Mr. PALKOVIC. It's a fascinating question because I think the arrival of the Internet has allowed the digitalization of any form of content to include video distribution over networks that were unimagined in serving that purpose.

That's why you see the excitement around companies like Netflix who've had a 230 percent increase in their stock price and have 44 million subscribers, more than any multichannel provider in the United States today, as well as innovations like Hulu and Roku and Amazon Prime, and VUDU, and other services.

I think you're going to see a much more multidimensional video marketplace; one with very nontraditional competitive forces coming from over-the-top alternatives, from companies who would have never been in the video business. You're seeing a flourishing in the program creation market with companies, again, like Netflix who can invest up to $100 million in original content. We're enjoying a relatively golden age of the creation of that content. And I, frankly, don't see anything that's going to stop the ability to field the incredible appetite Americans seem to have for high-quality television on any device they choose.

Senator PRYOR. Anybody else on the panel that would like to look into the crystal ball and see—yes. Yes, sir, Mr. Rogers.

Mr. ROGERS. It's a great question, Mr. Chairman.

We look at it this way. We think there's an ideal out there in terms of how the future of television is going to evolve and what we think that future is going to be is music.

The music industry got crushed by the onslaught of digital. But, with that, an entirely new model developed for consumers where, effectively, anything they want to get that's ever been written by way of song or music is available to any device they want. It follows them in the cloud; it can be personalized with playlists by genre; however they want it.

And most Americans have gotten to think that that is a great way to consume content. What we do is try to bring about that opportunity in the video realm without the incumbent business models being crushed. And that is, what we do is try to bring together, with a single box, a single remote, a single user interface, the ability to search across everything. Traditional video sources; your regular cable channels; your Video On Demand; and all the new offerings coming from the Internet, all coming together.

We're the only retail box that gives consumers that choice, that ability to say, "I know a great model out there; I want to apply it to television." And in so doing, we've been able to take that technology and build it out for cable operators so their boxes that they're providing that are not retail boxes can now provide that same degree of technology and ultimately that same consumer experience. If you take away this thing that sounds really unrelated but it's very related, how CableCARD exists to provide that competition, what you're going to do is undo the ability for that opportunity for consumers to have a great content consumption experience that we've built.

Senator PRYOR. Thank you.

Senator Smith.

Senator SMITH. Mr. Chairman, I think Michael is right. This is a very fast-evolving marketplace. It's already incredibly diverse. But I would simply note that in any given week, if you look at the top 100 shows, somewhere between 94 and 96 of them are broadcast content. It shows you where the eyeballs are.

And I would just simply make a plea on behalf of my members, both my networks that have expensive and highly-valued content that they have the right to control it and that they have the freedom to negotiate for its market value.

Senator PRYOR. Senator Wicker.

Senator WICKER. Well, thank you.

And I guess we could go on and on with that general question. Let me get down into the specific weeds. And, Mr. Powell and Mr. Rogers, see if I can get a conversation going between the two of you about the integration ban. And, you know, we're all consumers up here, too. So if you could sort of speak to us on the consumer level rather than as Senators or policymakers.

Mr. Powell, as I understand Mr. Rogers, he says that there's a better approach than CableCARDs. He sees a new approach that doesn't involve a physical card. They need time to establish this and that the House action, in repealing the FCC integration ban, is going to interfere with that. Now, I take it that you're quite satisfied with the approach of the House legislation with regard to the integration ban. Why is that good for consumers? And, what's wrong with what Mr. Rogers said about giving a little more leeway to get rid of this card but do the same thing for consumers?

Mr. POWELL. I'd make a couple critical points.

One, the legislation that we support in the House and the one that we would ask you to consider here does not, in any way, repeal Section 629 of the statute that requires the separate security requirement or require CableCARD. If you pass the legislation we are urging today, CableCARD would still be a solution that the FCC would still oversee, and they would still have a legal duty to continue to support.

What we had asked for is the removal of an FCC decision to include an integration ban requiring our boxes to use separate security. What that does is deny consumers a low-cost choice that could be created in the market. Meaning, if we're allowed to provide integrated security boxes that would be a low-cost option, among others, that consumers could choose.

I appreciate Mr. Rogers noting my laudatory comments as "God's machine" and I stand by them. It's a terrific device. The same year as Chairman of the FCC, a few years earlier, I dissented from this very rule because I believed it overstepped the bounds of Congress and wouldn't have the effect that it was intended.

So this would provide consumers another box of a different choice. It would also lower costs and lower energy consumption, CableCARD remains a solution, and future IP solutions, we believe, which we do agree, are due, we believe, can be developed in the marketplace.

Senator WICKER. The exact wording of the House Committee bill suits you fine. Is that right, Mr. Powell?

Mr. POWELL. Yes, sir, it does.

Senator WICKER. All right.

Now, Mr. Rogers, what's your response to Mr. Powell's position?

Mr. ROGERS. Well, the issue is: how do you preserve a retail market and the choice for cable subscribers which consumers have when it comes to smartphones or tablets, et cetera?

And, if you remove a common way for those devices to be developed around content security, which, in the end of the day has to do with can a consumer get access to the content that they want to buy their own box for. We've already seen, even under the CableCARD regime, cable operators who have tried to put in place technology that deny CableCARDs the ability to get a whole bunch of channels.

So if you went and bought a retail box, even under the CableCARD standard, it created a situation where cable companies were trying to thwart that and create a way for content channels to be distributed to their own boxes that retail boxes couldn't get. And if we hadn't scrambled and found a quick solution to that, there'd be no reason anybody would buy a retail box or that a competitive marketplace would develop. Because why would anybody do that if they couldn't get access to the cable content that they were subscribing to?

So CableCARDs have their flaws, what I'm just pointing to being one example. We've had our headaches with installation of CableCARDs. We're not sitting here saying that's the best system. There's an easy——

Senator WICKER. But the function needs to stay?

Mr. ROGERS. The function needs to stay.

The standard——

Senator WICKER. Mr. Lake?

Mr. ROGERS It doesn't require a regulation. It's the industry needs to come up with a replacement standard that applies to retail boxes and cable boxes, and then there's no issue. There's no cost or burden to the cable industry of what CableCARDs provide. It provides choice for consumers, and it allows the technology development that we stand for and the innovation that we stand for to thrive.

And we ask, why take off a current standard which is just going to end up bulkanizing the industry. Different companies; different solutions. We can't create a retail national device based on a hodge-podge of different standards. We need a single standard. And the industry could easily come up with one if policymakers said figure this out, figure it out quickly. Everybody wants to get rid of CableCARD, but we're not going to get rid of it until a new standard is in place.

Senator WICKER. Mr. Lake, help us out here. Which is the best way for us to protect the consumer here?

Mr. LAKE. We think the CableCARD regime has not been a full success in generating a robust retail market. It does have to be replaced for an IP delivery world, which is coming very quickly. We agree with that. When a replacement is worked out, we do think that the common reliance principle is a useful one to ensure that the cable companies have an incentive to support the technology that's used in retail boxes.

Senator WICKER. Thank you.

And thank you, Mr. Chairman.

Senator PRYOR. Senator Johnson.

STATEMENT OF HON. RON JOHNSON, U.S. SENATOR FROM WISCONSIN

Senator JOHNSON. Thank you, Mr. Chairman.

Being relatively new to this process here, not having been watching it for decades, this gets confusing very quickly.

Mr. Wood, you talked about JSAs, that they don't really meet the standard of good faith negotiation. Can you explain that to me?

Mr. WOOD. Well, the FCC, yesterday, decided that joint retransmission between allegedly separate licensees is a violation of that good faith bargaining duty because it allows a single entity, a single broadcaster, to control the negotiations for more than one broadcast outlet in the same market. And that leads to, according to small cable operators who typically serve rural customers and don't get quite the same discounts that the largest cable operators get, leads them to provide us with evidence that rates go up in that circumstance, those rates flow on to consumers. And that's why we're concerned about it just as the cable industry itself is.

Senator JOHNSON. Mr. Smith, can you give us your perspective on that?

Senator SMITH. Senator Johnson, there are two issues. One is joint selling of advertising. And the other is negotiating.

Very often, when my members negotiate with my friends here, they ask us to get together just out of economies of scale. I have a few members who argue about our ability to jointly negotiate.

When it comes to joint selling I would just simply note that I'd wish it on cable they do the same thing. But, it's applied only to us. It does not seem fair. And I don't mean to offend my friend, Bill Lake, here, but the FCC is under statutory obligation to do a biannual review of ownership in this vastly changing market. Do you know how long it's been since they've done that? Since 2007.

And so, do my members try to deal with the market realities that are out there? Of course they have. In order to promote localism, promote local news and weather, and especially emergency information, typically when there's a tornado bearing down on your community, it actually helps. The record is replete with how this has expanded with localism and diversity. And yet, we're singled out. It doesn't seem right. And it does seem a dereliction of duty on the part of the FCC to be square with broadcasting because there's no replacement for localism than us.

And when it comes to a lot of these issues, like distance signals, we want them to have it. STELA has lapsed before, in 2009. We kept their signals up. We want them to have those signals. But the question is shouldn't you want, as a matter of public policy, localism? Why do you want LA news brought into Wisconsin? They need to build out their networks——

Senator JOHNSON. We're veering off the subject of the joint sales agreements.

To me, personally, there's a great deal of bias toward the status quo. People base business models on that and then all of a sudden they get changed, possibly not following the statute.

Mr. Powell, can you just kind of speak to that? The stability of you've got a regulation people base their business models on, now the FCC is changing them without giving, I think what some people may consider due notice, not really following the statute in terms of the review.

Mr. POWELL. Let me be clear, at least representing the position of cable, because Gordon has raised it. We have no opinion whatsoever on the efficacy of joint sales in sales agreements. We haven't challenged that function; we don't have an opinion on that function.

I will note, however, that the accusation that what cable does is exactly the same as what broadcasting does is fundamentally different. The difference being that in these interconnect situations in which cable companies negotiate for advertising, you're talking about companies who are not competitors. They're in no way competitors with each other. In the context of broadcasting, they're companies that are otherwise supposedly competitors which raises other sets of concerns of which I've never examined, I don't have an opinion.

I do believe the FCC has an obligation to provide clear notice of what it's doing. But I really don't take an opinion on the dispute they're having with broadcasters over the local ownership rules.

Senator JOHNSON. Well, again, having been with the FCC, did you think the FCC was—did they overstep their bounds here in this latest decision?

Mr. POWELL. With the decision they made that concerns our issue, I don't believe they've overstepped their bounds at all. I think they had the obligation for decades to make sure that the good faith provision of retransmission consent is fully utilized and fully understood. And I think that their decision to prohibit joint negotiations in the top four is a natural extension of that authority.

Senator JOHNSON. OK.

My time is up, I guess, Mr. Smith.

Senator SMITH. I would just note, for the record, Senator Johnson, that by my count, 85 joint sales service agreements have already been approved by the FCC that are now disallowed and have to be unwound.

How do you attract investment to an industry when your regulator can change the rules ex post facto? A great injustice has been done to a lot of what has been done and the FCC is already blessed.

Senator JOHNSON. OK. Thank you, Mr. Chairman.

Senator PRYOR. Senator Ayotte.

STATEMENT OF HON. KELLY AYOTTE, U.S. SENATOR FROM NEW HAMPSHIRE

Senator AYOTTE. Thank you, Mr. Chairman. I want to thank the witnesses for being here. If we don't reauthorize STELA, what happens to my constituents in New Hampshire who rely on imported distant signals? And since STELA is a regulation, if it lapses is there an alternative marketplace mechanism to serve those viewers?

I would pose that to Senator Smith or anyone else on the panel who would like to comment.

Senator SMITH. Senator Ayotte, STELA has lapsed before and the signal stayed up. But we should be clear, that there's a reason why my friends in satellite, we want them to succeed, but they want this bill reauthorized so they don't have to buildup their network in order to provide your constituents local television. So they don't have to negotiate for retrans. They're exempted from that. So it's a subsidy that exists for the second and third largest pay-TV providers in the country.

Senator AYOTTE. Would anyone else on the panel like to comment?

Mr. WOOD. I would take issue with that, Senator, with some of those characterizations. I think that if the testimony and the materials that were prepared in response to the Committee's questions are correct, that DISH is serving every local market with local signals. And DirecTV, and Mr. Palkovic can correct me if I'm wrong, is serving all but a few of them. And many of your constituents are probably getting local signals from Boston or from New Hampshire stations depending on where they are within the state.

This provision, reauthorizing that, simply allows those who get distant signals from another city to continue receiving those. And I wouldn't really characterize it as a subsidy or as a regulation, but rather, a statutory license and limitation on certain rights under copyright law that broadcast stations have.

I appreciate Senator Smith saying they want those signals to stay on the air, but this is the mechanism that ensures that and keeps those signals on the air for your constituents.

Senator AYOTTE. I'm trying to understand if we don't reauthorize, what is the alternative? I understand, Senator Smith, what you're saying about the buildout and the investment that you believe needs to be made. I want to hear the panel's opinion on how you think this would occur? Let's assume we didn't reauthorize and how quickly could that occur? And, during that period, how do I say to my constituents that are receiving these distant signals, that while we're waiting for this investment to happen, that they won't be cut off? So, this is an important question for everyone up here.

Mr. PALKOVIC. Yes.

I'll speak on behalf of DIRECTV and DISH. I mean, we would not be allowed to continue to provide those signals to a million and a half customers or we'd be in violation of the law.

So there is no other alternative for those folks since they were prequalified as not being able to receive the off-air signal based on certain tests. And the tests are actually fairly outdated but if they were brought up to kind of the current standard of reality of what's going on out there, there would actually be even more people that would probably qualify.

With that said, we would have to take the signals away and they'd have no choice but to put an off-air antenna, which the very idea of that is kind of frustrating for them because that's what qualified them to get these signals in the first was they weren't able to receive the signal. So the fact that it's free over the air, does not mean that everybody is able to get a valid signal in the marketplace.

Senator AYOTTE. Senator Smith.

Senator SMITH. He's right about that, Senator Ayotte. Let me admit there are some narrow circumstances where this ought to be given to them and given to them permanently. But, there is an incentive built into this for them not to build out because they don't have to negotiate for a local retran.

And I think, for purposes if you want to foster localism, if you want your constituents to see news about your activities here as opposed to someone in California or New York, they ought to be encouraged to do that and make it permanent because there are some limited circumstances where a distant signal is necessary.

Mr. PALKOVIC. Just on that point, for the record, and Mr. Wood commented on this, DISH provides and has spent, between the two companies, we've spent billions of dollars on satellites and broadcast centers and uplink centers to provide service to just those 210 DMAs; 100 percent of them. We're 197 out of 210, which is 98 percent of the customers. So, yes, we're a few markets short and we have off-air antenna solutions currently being marketed in every one of those markets.

So the idea that we're not taking this seriously to try and avoid retrans consent is ridiculous. We've spent billions of dollars to do just the opposite.

Senator AYOTTE. Well, I really appreciate all of your answers on this. And it seems to me that if we were going down the road in terms of changing the mechanism now that there would need to be some kind of off-ramp or transition period because I am concerned about these consumers who are caught in the middle in terms of where we would be because of the regulatory framework. I think that would be a concern of many of us up here.

I thank you all for your testimony today.

Senator PRYOR. Thank you.

Senator Nelson.

STATEMENT OF HON. BILL NELSON, U.S. SENATOR FROM FLORIDA

Senator NELSON. It's so good to have a panel of such unanimity of opinion.

[Laughter.]

Senator NELSON. Well, two of the most frequent complaints that we get are cost and the blackouts. As a matter of fact, just for cost, for example, you've had the cable and other TV services have increased 6 to 7 percent over the last few years while the rate of inflation is 1.5 percent. A magazine did a study, *Consumer Reports,* and over a 15-year period, the difference over inflation was $1,750 for the cost versus the rise of inflation. Now, I know part of that answer is, well, there are additional services that you offer and so forth and I'd like anybody who would like to comment on it. This is a complaint that we get from consumers.

We also get a complaint from consumers when suddenly there is this showdown at high noon in the middle of the street, and the Super Bowl or whatever is a most-acclaimed show is suddenly going to be blacked out. Now, that's clearly not in the interest of the American public.

So tell us.

Senator SMITH. Senator Nelson, let me just say that I think the industry that I represent has done a poor job of educating the American consumers that when they buy a television set, there's an antenna in there and all they've got to do is plug it in. I just did that on ours. I get 39 stations here.

We are always on. There's never a blackout. And consumers, we need to educate them better. But we become the heavy in this that somehow we're to blame. You've just decided the *Consumer Reports* article, which I would recommend to all of you, broadcasters only barely begin to get retransmission consent for their highly-valued content since 2006. And it's hard. It's easy to show a thousand percent increase when you start from zero. But, what does broadcasting represent on a dollar of a cable bill? It represents two cents.

Senator NELSON. All right. Let me get Mr. Powell to answer.

Mr. POWELL. I would highlight two things for you when you look at rates over time. One, for example, the enormous explosion in channels and services that consumers subscribe to. For example, in 1995, if you look over that period, there were probably on average 24 channels offered to consumers on cable systems and we paid roughly $7 to acquire that, those 24 channels of content. By 2013, the average offered is closer to 100 channels and they are offered, I'm sorry, over 100 channels are offered and we pay about $34 per subscriber for that content.

And, I have to say, in response to Mr. Smith, it's all great and well to celebrate what's available for free. If that were really the driving force behind these businesses, we wouldn't hear about escalating retransmission fees, which, last year, increased 38 percent, predicted to increase 30 percent——

Senator NELSON. Let me interrupt you because we're running out of time.

Now Mr. Rogers disagrees with both of you because he says he can handle it all.

Mr. ROGERS. I think, Senator, the best antidote for price issues is competition. And, allowing consumers to show up with their own set-top box to be able to get just over-the-air signals, if that's all they want, or over-the-air signals and cable and Internet. We have shown that a consumer can save $500 or more over the life of a set-top box, if given the ability to show up with their own device.

The most galling thing to me in this whole debate is that while the FCC has established this scheme for a retail set-top box market to create competition, consumer choice, and, ultimately, have that kind of impact on price. There are regulations in place which tell cable operators if somebody shows up with your own box, then they're supposed to get a discount on the bundle that they pay $80 a month, $100 a month, by virtue of the fact that they're not getting a box from the cable operator; they're providing their own.

Senator NELSON. OK.

Mr. ROGERS. We are finding, far more often than not, that discount isn't being given. So somebody's being double-charged. That's something that really needs to be pressed.

Senator NELSON. Final question, Mr. Lake.

Mr. LAKE. Yes sir.

Senator NELSON. Is all of this an academic discussion because is the Internet cloud going to take it all over anyway?

Mr. LAKE. Well, we certainly believe that competition is the key. You've probably heard my Chairman say, more than once that his motto is "competition, competition, competition." We are trying to encourage competition in every part of this ecosystem as the best means of driving down prices.

Our action yesterday with respect to retransmission consent was in that theme. We were basically telling two competing stations you can't agree not to compete on retransmission fees. For that reason, we welcome over-the-air competition in video. That's just one more source of consumer choice and one more source of competition that will keep rates down.

Senator SMITH. Senator Nelson.

Senator NELSON. Mr. Chairman, my time is up. But, I want Mr. Lake to answer the question for the record, if he would, because here we are in a changing-daily technology and who knows how these services are going to be offered in the future. And I would like for the FCC to look ahead.

Senator PRYOR. Answer the question about the——

Senator NELSON. Thank you.

Senator PRYOR. Go ahead.

Mr. LAKE. We'd be happy to submit something.

Senator WICKER. Well, you know——

Senator PRYOR. Yes. Would you like to—go ahead and answer it now.

Senator WICKER.—consent he have another 2 minutes to actually answer the question?

Senator PRYOR. Sure.

Mr. LAKE. Yes.

Well, I think I was trying to get to that with the last part of that answer. We see now a tremendous source of competition for the video marketplace from the Internet; not only the wired Internet but also with LTE on the wireless side, the source of competition from the wireless side. And we do think that this will change a lot of the business models. We're already seeing a world in which there is at least some decline in pay-TV subscription because of these additional sources of competition.

And we don't know exactly where the marketplace will go and I think we aren't in a position to try to regulate its future but I think we do anticipate that there will be more consumer choice and more competition going forward. And that, ultimately, is the answer to higher prices.

Senator WICKER. And, Senator Smith.

Senator SMITH. I just think it's really important to point out something I'm not sure I fully grasped when I sat among you. To Senator Nelson's question: will the Internet take it all over? And the answer to that question is it can't by virtue of the laws of physics.

The distribution of wireless broadband is a one-to-one communication. Broadcasting is one-to-everyone in the demographic. The architectures are fundamentally different. And when you try to run all of the video through the Internet, guess what happens? It crashes. And in an emergency, do you want to crash? That's why broadcasting must be, as a matter of policy, a survivor industry in this because our architecture is irreplaceable by broadband. And it's physics. It isn't the laws of the regulations at the FCC or the laws of Congress. It's the laws of physics.

Senator PRYOR. Mr. Wood, just 30 seconds then we have to go to our next question.

Mr. WOOD. Yes, very briefly. Thank you, Senator.

I often talk about the model that Chairman Powell described as, when we're providing more channels, look at all the value they make you buy. I think that the ultimate answer to the price increases you talked about, Senator, and to the blackouts as well, is giving people more choice about what to buy both online and on their pay-TV platform so that they actually have some view of what those retransmission—thank you, Senator. What those retransmission consent bills mean for them. And also, what cable channels and online options mean to them, as well, for the bill they pay at the end of the month.

Senator PRYOR. I'll give others a chance to respond to that in a moment. But, Senator Klobuchar, I know that you need to ask. Go ahead.

STATEMENT OF HON. AMY KLOBUCHAR, U.S. SENATOR FROM MINNESOTA

Senator KLOBUCHAR. Well, thank you very much. I appreciate Senator Blunt allowing me to go first. I have some veterans visiting from Minnesota up there. So thank you.

And thank you for holding this very important hearing, Chairman Pryor. And it's the only way that many of the 650,000 satellite subscribers in our state can get access to video services is through satellite; 34 million nationwide. I have the honor of being one of three Senators, including Senator Cruz, to be on both the Judiciary and Commerce Committee. So this will be my second opportunity to talk about STELA. Very exciting.

OK. So I thought I would start with you, Mr. Palkovic. You weren't at our last hearing. And, is reauthorization of this act still necessary to ensure satellite continues to be competitive with cable? And, specifically, how has Section 119, which is expiring in the permanent Section 122, impacted your ability to compete in the video marketplace?

Mr. PALKOVIC. There's no question it has given us the ability to compete. And I think, based on my prior comments, the reason we made those investments between ourselves and DISH is because that programming is invaluable to consumers. And, any way you can get it to them is important to them; whether it's through satellite, whether it's cable, whether it's over the air. If they can't get it through the over-the-air model that was originally designed, they should be allowed to get it through the STELA Act. So it's critical that we reauthorize this.

Senator KLOBUCHAR. Are there any changes, you think, since 2010, that's made a difference in how we reauthorize it?

Mr. PALKOVIC. Since 2010?

Senator KLOBUCHAR. Yes.

Mr. PALKOVIC. I think this is the opportunity to make those changes. I was going to finish this by saying it's all the more reason why if it's such important programming to consumers, as Honorable Smith stated several times today, then don't black it out. Don't use that as kind of a bully negotiating tactic. Negotiate, you know, straight up with your distributers without bringing the consumers into it. That's the part that we object most to.

Senator KLOBUCHAR. Senator Smith, I asked this question to Ms. Burdick during the Judiciary Hearing but wanted to extend it to you, as well, if you have anything to add. During the last STELA reauthorization, we had a lot of concerns about orphan counties, and these were defined for local broadcasters about the way the DMAs were defined. And this is an issue I spoke about during the Judiciary markup and in the Commerce Committee's consideration of STELA 5 years ago. Can you discuss how DMAs are still important for local advertising and local economies?

Senator SMITH. Absolutely.

Your local commerce needs to have a local out-web and that is broadcasting. That's none of these national providers.

And so, I just think it's absolutely fundamental that we be included in this. And you ask if STELA—what would happen? Look, we both have an incentive to make sure our stuff is on their satellites. We want that to happen. So when it lapsed before, it continued on because we both have equal incentive to make sure viewers get their local TV. We just think it's better local than a distant signal from the major markets on the coast.

Senator KLOBUCHAR. OK, thank you.

Mr. Rogers, a little different question. Why isn't there more competitive market or products that connect to cable systems? What do you think we could do to spur competition?

Mr. ROGERS. It's a great question. Well, certainly a new standard that's a better standard than CableCARDs where key industry players agree to what that standard ought to be.

Two, I think it should include all cable content. That was one of the mistakes the FCC made in limiting the kind of content, the kind of channels, that a retail set-top box would be able to access. Certainly, it needs to provide for the fact there'll be this transition to IP technology and to incorporate a standard that fully allows a retail set-top box to develop with IT. Consider the opportunity to bring in all providers of video and not necessarily just cable in terms of access to signals, because I think that will provide the most competition and choice for all consumers.

Senator KLOBUCHAR. Very good.

Just one last question here, Mr. Powell. Our reauthorization of STELA includes reauthorizing the good faith standard requiring both broadcasters and all multichannel video programming distributers to negotiate in good faith for the retransmission consent. Do you believe this is working?

Mr. POWELL. I would emphasize, I do think it's a critical, mutual obligation on both parts particularly if we're concerned about the dangers that retransmission consent has to lead to blackouts. So I would encourage its reauthorization for as long as possible.

I think it's been underutilized. I think it has been underutilized by the FCC and I'm proud to see Chairman Wheeler, yesterday, taking steps to get meaningful content by preventing joint negotiations of retransmissions consent. So I do believe it's an effective provision. It's a provision that probably could be used more fully to try and protect consumers in these commercial negotiations.

Senator KLOBUCHAR. One last thing.

We're going to have, as you know, next week, Mr. Palkovic in the Judiciary Committee on the Comcast-Time Warner merger. You're aware of that; right?

Mr. PALKOVIC. I have not heard about that. Is that in the House?

Senator KLOBUCHAR. OK.

[Laughter.]

Senator KLOBUCHAR. Well, I just wandered if you had any views on this or you prefer to put them in writing on the merger? Since you're sitting here.

Mr. PALKOVIC. Yes, since I'm sitting right here.

Well, look, there are a lot of issues that we're very interested in and some we're concerned about, but we have not taken a public position on any of them yet. We are looking at it very seriously, though, back with the folks on, you know, the executive team and the right folks on this.

When we're ready, and we have a position, we'll come out with it in the proper channels.

Senator KLOBUCHAR. Appreciate it, thank you.

And thank you, Mr. Chairman. And thank you, Senator Blunt.

Senator PRYOR. Thank you.

Let's see. We will go Senator Blunt, Senator Thune, Senator McCaskill, and then Senator Cruz.

STATEMENT OF HON. ROY BLUNT, U.S. SENATOR FROM MISSOURI

Senator BLUNT. Thank you, Chairman.

Mr. Lake, last week, and in the last couple of weeks, I've sent two letters to the FCC urging the Commission to carry out its comprehensive media ownership reviews before acting on any rule changes impacting Joint Sales Agreements. I do know that in both the Joplin market and the Springfield market that I used to represent in the House of Representatives, that in each of those markets they have Joint Sales Agreements.

When you were talking on the topic just a moment ago, you talked about increased competition for the video marketplace. Frankly, if you'd been defending the old rule that allowed these kinds of agreements, that would've been the perfect way to competition.

I have a couple of questions. One is Commissioner Pai has said that he didn't think there was an adequate review of how this would impact minority-owned and women-owned stations that had a disproportional number of these Joint Agreements. And so, one question is going to be, I'll ask a couple here in a row, was there a review that, the kind of review I asked for, that would have got all the information that two of the other Commissioners say you didn't have? And two, in reviewing agreements that are already in place, I think you've given yourself 90 days to do that and are you going to stick with that 90-day review standard? And, will you have any special consideration for agreements that have been previously approved and a significant number of business decisions made based on what the FCC told these stations operating under Joint Agreements they could do?

Mr. LAKE. Yes.

As to your first question, we think Commissioner Pai's concern is misplaced. We do have a substantial amount of information. We have seen over the last decade, and particularly in the last several years, a tremendous upsurge in the number of Joint Sales Agreements that stations are using.

As you know, we have rules limiting the number of stations that can be co-owned in a local market. And what we've seen is a growing use of Joint Sales Agreements; all of them we've seen in recent years are for a 100 percent of the advertising of the sidecar station. They're typically joined with a number of other types of financial and other entanglements and what we concluded was that these were basically causing the equivalent of ownership of a station that was nominally independently owned.

We're not the only to reach that conclusion. The Justice Department treats these sidecar stations as owned when it does merger reviews. And the companies themselves, when they report to the Securities and Exchange Commission, treat these as basically the same as their owned stations.

So we have a situation in which we haven't yet completed the quadrennial review to consider what the rules should be, but——

Senator BLUNT. Were any of these Joint Management Agreements allowed without the FCC agreeing that they could go forward?

Mr. LAKE. Excuse me?

Senator BLUNT. Weren't these all approved by the FCC when they moved forward?

Mr. LAKE. We don't approve agreements except in the context of transactions. We have approved a number of transactions in recent years that included JSAs. This was against a background in which the Commission proposed in 2004 to attribute them to treat them as ownership——

Senator BLUNT. Well, I'm going to run out of time here. So let me go to Senator Smith. I'll join the Chairman who welcomed you back to the Committee and certainly it's good to see you.

But do you want to comment on this from the station ownership perspective and the kind of interlocking financial arrangements which include borrowing money and doing things with that borrowed money that Mr. Lake suggested were out there?

Senator SMITH. If the FCC had any intention to damage broadcasting, they made a good start with what they did yesterday. It has dramatically damaged a number of broadcasting stocks; just check with Wall Street. But it just strikes me as fundamentally unfair when I know of 85 that they specifically blessed as not in any way violative of public policy but, in fact, the economies of scale— I'm not talking about negotiating that Michael mentioned. We can deal with that. But, in selling advertising. Those economies of scale have allowed the spreading of local news, weather and sports and, particularly, emergency information. Those are now all in jeopardy unless they grant, re-grant, what they've already granted.

But as to how I see this as unfair—and I'm certainly open to Michael to tell me how JSAs are somehow different than interconnects. I've got their advertisement right here. It says, "Interconnects are collections of two or more cable systems in a market working together to distribute commercials. Interconnects make it easy to plan and buy cable in local markets with only one buy, one commercial, and one invoice. An advertiser can reach an entire market full of cable homes with one call." Well, come on. Where is that fair? Both the damage to localism, the damage to broadcaster, the damage the deal is already done but permit it for our friends in cable.

Senator BLUNT. Chairman Powell, do you want to respond to that?

Mr. POWELL. The only thing——

Senator BLUNT. Senator Smith is still asking questions here in the Committee, you see.

Mr. POWELL. I remain intrigued why broadcasters insist on sort of impugning what we're doing given that we haven't in any way

62

suggested what they're doing is problematic. But since he has, I would note for you, and I can provide for the record, that the Department of Justice has reviewed these kinds of interconnect relationships and has found them to be acceptable buying groups, principally because the companies involved are not competitors of each other. That's a very significant difference under antitrust laws and concerns around collusive activities.

So all I can say is that the things that are being referenced have been reviewed, approved by Department of Justice at different times, and continue to involve very small cable companies that are not competitors with each other.

Senator BLUNT. I would just say, as I complete this thought, Chairman and to Mr. Lake, I think the Joint Sales Agreements that have been approved should be handled in a significantly different way. I don't believe I agree on your forward-going view of this either, but I would definitely disagree that you can go back and ask these stations to unwind business decisions that have been made for years relying on JSAs.

Mr. LAKE. If I could clarify what we've done with respect to that, the 90-day provision is the timetable that the Commission has set for the Media Bureau to consider applications for waiver.

But as to existing agreements, what the Commission has done is what it did when it attributed radio JSAs, which is to give a 2-year period for them to be unwound or adjusted to comply with the ownership rules.

Senator BLUNT. I'll have some more questions for the record.

Thank you, Chairman.

Senator PRYOR. Senator Thune.

STATEMENT OF HON. JOHN THUNE,
U.S. SENATOR FROM SOUTH DAKOTA

Senator THUNE. Thank you, Mr. Chairman.

I want to thank you and Senator Wicker for having this hearing as we head toward a STELA reauthorization and there are, as has already been pointed out, lots of moving parts on these issues.

I'd like to follow up on some things that were stated in the opening remarks. Mr. Powell, a question for you and then for Senator Smith. Senator Smith argued in his prepared testimony, and I quote, "The removal of broadcasters from the basic tier will have the certainly unintended effect of increasing cable bills for the subscribers who want their local broadcast channels."

Now, that doesn't sound like a good outcome, especially with cable rates that are already increasing every year. So the question is, without the basic tier mandates, would cable companies simply put local broadcast channels on higher tiers and effectively raise the rates on subscribers who want those channels?

Mr. POWELL. I think quite the contrary.

Under the retransmission consent regime, Congress has provided a broadcaster a choice. He can either be carried on a cable system under the must-carry provisions without compensation as a guaranteed right of law, or they can elect essentially to go on the free market, which is often a conversation that they insist on, were able to attain the value of the content that we believe it deserves.

In that free market, negotiating, in addition to price, the terms and conditions of carriage including placement should be something that someone believes that it can be fully compensated should be able to be achieved. I will tell you, in fact, a vast majority of cable agreements today, with broadcasters, often include contractual terms that provide for carriage on the basic tier.

I think it's anachronistic to say that you can negotiate supposedly in a free market for carriage, but the government has guaranteed you carriage on a particular tier and that the American consumer has to buy your product before being allowed to buy any other channel. I think if consumers were freed from that obligation, there would at least be the possibility to do the very thing Senator Smith talks about, which is put up an antenna, get those channels over the air for free, and not have to pay for them additionally as part of someone's cable subscription; which today, they have to do.

So I actually believe the prospects would be for the consumers' benefit rather than would have increased cost.

Senator THUNE. Senator Smith, Mr. Powell suggests, in his prepared testimony, that eliminating the basic tier purchase mandate, and I quote, "Would also mean that consumers would not have to pay for such broadcast stations as a condition of receiving cable service." And you previously testified before this committee that "nearly every major television broadcaster now provides its content to viewers in crystal clear high-definition over the air for free." That was a quote from you.

So the question is, do you believe that consumers should remain required by law to purchase the channels your members offer over the air for free in order to receive non-broadcast channels?

Senator SMITH. Senator Thune—and a perfect example that happened to a medium-sized market, Senator Johnson's city of Milwaukee, Journal of Broadcasting ran into a dispute with Time Warner Cable. A big company versus a little broadcaster. When it was settled, Time Warner had sold their place on the tier to the game show in which they had a financial interest.

Now, I can tell you that the basic tier, you know, was a benefit broadcasting got on the Cable Act as something of a compensation for all of the burdens of regulation apply only to us. And so, if you're going to relieve—take away one benefit, relieve some of the burden. But that really misses the point of why Congress put in the basic tier.

The basic tier was put in as a matter of public safety so that if an elder person in Joplin, Missouri has a tornado bearing down on them, they don't have to go to channel 750 or hunt for their local station. It's where they know it's been and it's for their convenience, not ours. So when you mess that, you know, it—look what happened in Milwaukee. Look what could happen if, all of the sudden, your CBS channel is in 450, or ABC channel is in the 800s, and NBC is in the 700s. And you got to start hunting. The basic tier is not about us; it's actually about public safety. Now, it applies only to cable. I don't wish them to have any regulations but, on the other hand, I'd simply want to remind the Committee why it was there in the first place.

Now, satellite provides a basic tier. They have no obligation to do that. And why did they do that? Because they need our stuff to sell their subscriptions. And their consumers need to know where ABC is, NBC is, CBS and FOX, so that their local channels are convenient to them.

Senator THUNE. Mr. Powell and Mr. Palkovic, Jay Huizenga, the General Manager of KELO Television in Sioux Falls, South Dakota, recently wrote in an op-ed, and I quote, "That it's only fair that the government allow broadcasters to negotiate for retransmission consent revenue." Do either of you disagree with that statement?

Mr. POWELL. No.

Mr. PALKOVIC. No.

Senator THUNE. Great.

Well, Mr. Chairman, I thank you and thank our panelists for sharing their testimony today.

Senator PRYOR. Thank you.

Senator McCaskill.

STATEMENT OF HON. CLAIRE McCASKILL, U.S. SENATOR FROM MISSOURI

Senator McCASKILL. Well, let me just say that listening to the testimony today, and knowing this Congress, I think that we should all go buy lotto tickets if we think we're going to come up with the STELA that's going to sail through the U.S. Senate, because it's a long shot.

But, I want to talk a little bit about consumers here and I really want to—we've covered a lot of ground on retransmission, and we've covered a lot of ground on basic tier, and channels merging. I'd like to talk about the business model that has consumers scratching their head all over the country. And that is the pricing and billing practices of satellite and cable.

You know, I don't think people realize. I want the word to go out right now. Call your provider today and find out what they're charging you that they shouldn't be charging you. Call every 6 months because that's the model that's out there. I discovered that I was paying extra for speed on an Internet that now was the basic speed. They were still charging me. And when I ask, "How could they do that?" They said, "Well you have to call in." I said, "Well I don't remember getting that in my bill that I should be calling in to check in case you're charging me for something that is now what everybody gets." Same thing with HD.

There are people out there who are paying an extra lug. It's not a lot; it's $4 or $5 on their bill, $10 on their bill. They don't even know perhaps that that provider has gone to all HD now and they're still paying that $10 every month and they'll pay it until they ask about it.

Now, how do you get away with that? How do we do that? I don't get it. I mean, I get it when you go to a car dealership, you're going to haggle over a price of a car, but I don't think the consumer is supposed to be giving me the directive that you've got to haggle over your cable bill or your satellite TV bill on a monthly basis. And then, this whole notion that we're going to give you now for this amount, but then, in 3 months, it's going to go to this amount, and then, in 6 months, it's going to go to this amount, and then, in a year, it's going to go to this amount, and, by the way, in 3 years it's going to go to this amount. But by the way, don't rely on any of that because it could change and, by the way, if you call you probably won't have to pay it.

Now who thought of this business model? And let me ask Mr. Lake, can the FCC do anything about this? It's ridiculous.

Mr. LAKE. We share your concern. With respect to——

Senator MCCASKILL. It's more than a concern. It infuriates me. Can't you tell?

Mr. LAKE. With respect to billing practices, we have authority to impose Truth-in-Billing requirements on voice services. We do not have the same authority with respect to cable or satellite services.

Senator MCCASKILL. So there's no authority anywhere to get after people who are charging people for something that they are getting at lower price if they just ask for it.

Mr. LAKE. Yes, there is.

As to basic cable service, I think the local franchising authorities have authority to regulate billing practices but the FCC does not.

Senator MCCASKILL. I'm going to give you guys a chance to respond.

Mr. PALKOVIC. Well, first of all, on behalf of DIRECTV, that is not our practice; to intentionally, knowingly, go out and do what you just described. In fact, it's more often the case that when we have the opportunity to change our pricing and prices go down, generally speaking, that's adjusted downward for any affected customers.

Senator MCCASKILL. Without them having to call you?

Mr. PALKOVIC. Without them having to call us.

Now, there are, as you can imagine, I think there's indirectly because of the series of acquisitions with PrimeStar and their pricing and packaging and USSB over the years, we have over 2,000 different package prices in our billing system that we have to communicate to the 20 million customers. Most of those are there, the term grandfathering is used, so that we introduce a new package, we don't bring customers up to the new price which would be a price increase. We leave them down at the price that they'd agreed to. Now, both of those customers may get an annual increase but more often than not, and I would say, you know, in a business like ours where there are that many transactions, you're going to make some mistakes and when we find them and they're pointed out to us, we correct them immediately.

We take taking care of the consumer extremely serious at DIRECTV. In fact, that's the entirety of my job. I run all the call centers and all the technicians. I have 40,000 people that get up every day in this country to work on the consumer. So it's my job to make sure that we don't do what you just described.

There are, undoubtedly, people out there that are either flip about it, or careless, or lazy but we are not one of those. We take what you just said very seriously. We're actually spending in the magnitude of about $20 million today to do nothing more than create a very simple, transparent, consumer-friendly bill that we're going to introduce this year. Our bill was technically correct but it was very confusing. That's a lot of money to spend to keep sending a bill out just to make sure they don't misunderstand it.

Senator MCCASKILL. Right.

Well, I know, Mr. Powell, that it's difficult for you to respond and I'll ask you to respond for the record. But let me briefly, I know I'm out of time, don't you think that if we went to an à la carte system, Senator, that you would compete very well on an à la carte system?

I know on all the channels that people get, I have a sense that they would want to buy their local channels for the local content. And is there any reason—let me just ask you this—does anybody think that we will go to a complete à la carte system as a business model anytime in the next decade?

Just say yes, if you think that we will.

Does anybody think that we'll go to an à la carte business model without being forced to by government intervention any time in the next 20 years?

Mr. POWELL. Senator, I don't.

Senator MCCASKILL. No?

Mr. WOOD. I would just point out, Senator, that the bills that we have supported would not require à la carte alone but would require an à la carte option to be made available to people. So that's why we think that by allowing bundling, of course, it's something that some people will want to choose. They want to have that package but we want people to have the choice if they want to buy individual channels to make that decision themselves.

Senator MCCASKILL. Thank you.

Senator SMITH. Senator McCaskill, I would just simply say, if I may, Mr. Chairman, yes, we'd do very well under à la carte, but some of my members don't support à la carte and others do support à la carte. And my counsel would advise me to invoke my constitutional right against self-incrimination if I take a position on à la carte.

Senator MCCASKILL. All right.

Senator PRYOR. Senator Cruz.

STATEMENT OF HON. TED CRUZ,
U.S. SENATOR FROM TEXAS

Senator CRUZ. Thank you, Mr. Chairman, and I appreciate the Subcommittee holding this hearing. I appreciate all the witnesses being here. There's a lot of expertise here today and I appreciate your time and good counsel.

Since 1998, Congress has reauthorized legislation like this every 5 years, continually making changes to these laws. And they seem to get more and more complicated. As a lawyer who spent a number of years in private practice, I can certainly say that these laws are among the most complicated laws that the legal system faces and, indeed, courts struggle to interpret them.

The question I'd like to ask the panel is, is rather than continually adding conditions, adding mandates, adding complexity, is there not a path we could go on to subtract from the complexity to make it simpler to allow free negotiations between large mature competitive industries? These are not startups anymore. These are mature industries. And I'd welcome the panel's collective views on if the direction, the one-way ratchet of more and more complexity, more and more burdens can be turned the other way?

Senator SMITH. Senator Cruz, if I may?

67

We've testified that we just as soon see it go. We're very anxious to keep our signals on satellite. We want people to get our content. We want to be fairly compensated. We have the ability to negotiate for that.

For us, STELA is—but I will repeat: there are some that would be orphaned that should be permanently made available. But, for us, the 5-year STELA is like every five years it's a chance to harpoon the broadcasters when they swim by. There's nothing in it for us here. This is just what we can take away from broadcasters, what we can add to in terms of more burdens and regulations.

Mr. ROGERS. Senator, at TiVo, our view is that there shouldn't be anything by way of additional legislation. Our view is that, just to your point, there ought to be a way for industries to work this out on a voluntary basis; that if the existing regulatory regime that applies to this area is lifted after the industries have been told, "Look, go work this out. Make sure there's competition for consumers. Make sure there's a non-burdensome standard for cable operators. Make sure there's a good way for the kind of technology that we deliver is easily ported for cable operators." That can probably be done. Done relatively quickly. And, as a result, we don't see any need for legislation to address this area at all.

Mr. WOOD. I would say, Senator just to the point about adding burdens to broadcasters, in 2010, the reauthorization actually required people to take their local broadcast signals if they wanted to continue receiving these distant signals. So with respect to satellite provisions alone, I would dispute the notion that somehow they're particularly aimed at broadcasters by reducing their rates or reducing their carriage.

On the complexity point, we were talking about this earlier with Senator Ayotte as well, and I think there are ways to reduce the complexity but, as I said in my testimony, not piecemeal; not to simply say, "Well, let's let this statutory license expire and see what happens. But rather, to overhaul copyright entirely." And, Senator, Chairman Rockefeller talked about the communications rewrite, it's always just around the corner, I'm sure the copyright rewrite is always just around the corner, too. But that's the kind of path we would like to see as a comprehensive solution rather than just letting certain provisions go away.

Mr. POWELL. Senator, recently I testified in the House on the future of telecom deregulation and the entire theme of the testimony was simplicity, what we titled it. I commend it to you. I'd be happy to send it to your office because I do think we're dealing with a statutory regime that's 750,000 words and it's premised at a time and a place where the market was radically different than it is today.

Just by virtue of one illustration, 1992 Cable Act, the cable industry represented well over 90 percent of all multichannel video production. Today, we represent only 50 percent. Back then, we were vertically integrated over 50 or 60 percent with content. Today, that's down to less than 12 percent of content. Yet, there are many rules that are built on those underlying premises.

The bottom line is there are a lot of companies that can take care of their own interests and the market is fast-moving and innovative. It's why we raise questions about provisions like must-buy which really provide a unique advantage to one set of very significant companies. By the way, if it's so harmful, 50 percent of the market aren't subject to the rule. All of the third and fourth largest providers in the country aren't subject to the must-buy rule. Yet, the cable industry is.

These are prunings that need to happen to simplify and better level the playing field.

Senator CRUZ. And, Mr. Chairman, my time has expired but if I could ask one additional question. And, this is addressed to Mr. Lake. After there was a large public outcry, and a significant outcry from Congress, the FCC has announced that it has discontinued its plans with regard to its critical information needs study, which would have inserted government observers into newsrooms.

Mr. Lake, what I would ask you today, and let me say I was one of those deeply concerned about that proposed plan, can you assure this committee today that the FCC has no intention to go forward with this kind of inquiry either through the CIN or any other similar course?

Mr. LAKE. I should say that the intrusion into the newsrooms was not an intended aspect of that study. When that issue was brought to the Commission's attention it did abandon the study. I know of no plans to continue with a study of that type.

Senator CRUZ. Well, thank you. And let me encourage you in having no plans to do so.

Thank you, Mr. Chairman.

Senator PRYOR. Thank you.

Senator Markey, is it true that you wrote the Satellite Television Bill shortly after they sent Sputnik up?

[Laughter.]

STATEMENT OF HON. EDWARD MARKEY, U.S. SENATOR FROM MASSACHUSETTS

Senator MARKEY. We had an era.

I'll tell you what happened. You know, I campaigned for my candidate for President in 1980 in Iowa and 1988 in Iowa. And, I'm a former future cabinet officer in many administrations.

[Laughter.]

Senator MARKEY. But I learned a lot about Iowa. I learned a lot about Iowa.

And we had these huge eight foot dishes and basketball courts and farms. And I would ride through, and I'd say, There's got to be a way that these dishes are not eight feet wide." You know? And so, that is what the 1992 Cable Act is all about. It's the 18-inch satellite dish industry which is, if nothing else, an incredible addition to the aesthetic quality of our Nation. OK?

[Laughter.]

Senator MARKEY. And so, yes, I was there at day one and that was my bill back then long ago and far away. So thank you, Mr. Chairman.

So, welcome. You know, that was 22 years ago and the Satellite Home Viewer Act, which eventually became STELA, allowed satellite companies to transmit broadcast signals. And we had a revolution going. And now, 34 million Americans have 18-inch satellite dishes.

And moving forward, satellite service should remain a vital competitor in the pay-TV market for consumers. And, as we begin debate on the reauthorization of STELA, we should evaluate whether any proposed change to STELA would promote competition consumer choice in the public interest. That's what we did when we put those laws on the books, telecommunications a generation ago.

So I would like to, if I could, move to a set-top box issue because that was a provision in the 1996 STELA Communications Act, which I was the author of along with Tom Bliley, who was a Republican from Virginia and the Chairman of the Commerce Committee in the House, which was really aimed at unleashing competition and innovation in the retail marketplace, enabling consumers to buy the set-top box of their choice independent of their network provider making the consumer king. And that bill passed through this committee and through the House committee in 1996.

And, in the age of the Smartphone, we should think of these devices as smart video boxes. The devices that, ideally, would help consumers navigate to the video and information sources of their choice. So 18 years have passed since the 1996 Telecom Act and it's clear that over these two decades the promise of a robust dynamic smart video box retail market has largely been unfulfilled. And it's true that the market has changed since the 1990s and I'm open-minded about how we continue to push policies that promote competition.

I think we have to accept changes in technology, but we have to make sure that nothing that happens limits the choices of consumers. OK? I think we should also agree with that. The consumer should be king. That was my vision then and it remains to be my vision today, especially in a multichannel video programming world.

So I'll start with you, Mr. Rogers. I think we can all agree that we should not be wed to CableCARD; that we need to move on to the next technology. But what would you suggest that we do with the cable industry in order to have a standard that ensures the consumers continue to be able to purchase their own navigation devices before we lift the integration ban? How do we do that?

Mr. ROGERS. Well, thank you, Senator.

The answer to that, I think, is clearly there is a downloadable security standard meaning software that can be downloaded that doesn't require a physical card and you get out from under that and you get out from under the cost to operators and the burdens that have been associated with it and you get out of the frustration for consumers and the frustrations that have been associated with installation of CableCARD. So we've got to get to a next generation standard.

If you get rid of the current standard before, meaning common reliance, meaning the cable operator and retail boxes have to be based on the same kind of content security, if you get rid of that before there's a new standard we've got no hope of getting to a new standard.

So I think this is not complicated. It's a relatively simple process. There are really a small number of cable operators. So, I think, sitting down with ourselves and any other company that would like to do what we do, and come up with a downloadable security system that can become that national standard to preserve retail choice. And once it's in place, once the FCC certifies it, I see no reason that CableCARDs can't be lifted. And I see that that whole process could take place pretty quickly but the idea—I'm sorry.

Senator MARKEY. OK. I thank you. So let me just move along quickly because I want to reach one other subject, if I could, retransmission consent and have a little discussion about that, with your indulgence, Mr. Chairman.

Again, retransmission consent goes back to the 1992 Cable Act, as well. And so, last August I was concerned by reports that amidst a retransmission dispute between CBS and Time Warner, CBS was blocking access to its Internet-based video for Time Warner Cable broadband customers. This blocking occurred even in cases where the consumer was not a Time Warner Cable video subscriber; meaning the consumer was only a Time Warner Cable broadband customer. I believe that the consumer's choice of cable television providers should not be tied to her ability to access Internet content that is freely available to other consumers.

Accordingly, I wrote a letter to the FCC, calling on the Commission to actively defend Internet freedom and consumer rights, and thankfully that dispute was resolved and access was restored.

Mr. Smith, I'd like to get your views on those issues, and you, Mr. Powell, and you, Mr. Lake, if we could.

With your indulgence, Mr. Chairman.

Senator PRYOR. Sure.

Senator SMITH. Senator, nice to see you.

Senator MARKEY. Thank you.

Senator SMITH. I think you were referring to the Time Warner/CBS shutdown. I'm not privy to those negotiations but from press reports what was clear is Time Warner was asking them for an exclusivity that would prevent CBS from negotiating carriage rights for its very valuable content with Netflix, Hulu, or whomever. And so, they took a tough stand and they won, ultimately, I think the outcome you would like, but at the time they had—they are tough negotiators and they defended their right to make sure that other newcomers online could negotiate with them.

Thank you.

Senator MARKEY. Mr. Powell.

Mr. POWELL. Senator, recently in our comments that we filed at the FCC under net neutrality, we alluded to the growing dangers that edge providers are those that control distribution and content have certainly the ability, power, and sometimes incentive to also disrupt consumer access to content. And that's an issue that certainly should be in the conversation around ensuring consumers have free and unfettered access to Internet content. So we think it's an issue worthy of consideration.

Senator MARKET. OK, good. Thank you.

And, Mr. Lake.

Mr. LAKE. That dispute illustrates the fact that retransmission consent negotiations are much more complex than they used to be. They now commonly include online rights. And, we've also seen a Disney-DISH deal that also involved online rights although it did not involve a blackout. We worked very closely with both parties to that dispute. As you know, we have a responsibility to enforce the duty of negotiation in good faith and we worked with both companies at the highest management levels to try and encourage them to resolve that dispute. We're glad that it was finally resolved and that, at least by reports, it did not involve any exclusive online rights.

Senator MARKEY. And just again, it's another illustration of why we have to be so careful in what we're doing with technologies' change, but the values have to stay the same; the goals that we have have to stay the same. And we have to make sure that those goals, competition, consumer choice are there because that ultimately is what makes us the leader in the world on these issues.

And, I thank you, Mr. Chairman.

Senator PRYOR. Thank you very much.

And let me just follow up on one thing. We've talked a little bit about the CableCARD but someone mentioned, I think it was you, Mr. Powell, in passing you said something about the energy usage of the CableCARD and you threw out a big figure, I think. I think it was you, but——

Mr. POWELL. Yes, sir.

Senator PRYOR.—I'm curious about why it uses so much energy and where do we get those numbers. I know it's kind of minor but I am curious.

Mr. POWELL. I can provide details for the record but the citation is the EPA found that CableCARDs add an additional 15 kilowatts of power as an energy consumption when they're separated in that manner. And so, the additional burden of running leased set-top boxes that don't have any technical need for a separate security requirement amounts to, when you add it up, over 500 kilowatts of additional energy expense to the American consumer without any—to the consumer. That's all I was referring to was the EPA estimates that are in their citation.

Senator PRYOR. Mr. Rogers.

Mr. ROGERS. Just another example, Mr. Chairman, of innovation that we ported to the cable industry. What we allowed cable operators to do is take small IP set-top boxes with no CableCARDs that are linked to one primary set-top box and, with that, have the ability to get out of what used to be the only way to approach this which was multiple set-top boxes with multiple CableCARDs. So another reason energy conservation to get to another standard, a smarter standard, but along the way here we are contributing innovation that I think has contributed to what operators are able to do on that issue.

Senator PRYOR. Mr. Palkovic, were you going to say something? OK.

I do have a question for you, Mr. Palkovic. And that is, I think we've got through this whole hearing, maybe, without really talking about orphan counties and that issue that does come up with satellite. And I am wondering about your view of whether, you know, Congress maybe should try and address that in this reauthorization? And are we looking at a general systemic fix? Is that the best way to do it or is there another way that we should talk about it?

Mr. PALKOVIC. Well, first of all, I think we do agree it needs to be addressed. It's unfortunate, but the current map, you know, it's a map that Congress adopted, a Nielsen map, that's from the 1950s. So you will have a DMA that will, essentially, give somebody one state, will assign them as part of a DMA in another state. And I don't have a great example, but it's frustrating for those customers when the local channels that they're authorized to get, even if they receive them through us or DISH, are from a different state.

So, somehow we'd like to be able to offer consumers the right to choose the local channels from their state as an option. There's not that many of these people but it's very frustrating for them. Now we, I know, and DISH feels strongly the same way, would like to work together before we change any of the rules because we designed those billions of dollars of satellites.

I talked about our design around this mapping system with our spot beams. I mean, they're launched. You can't change those. So we'd have to be a little bit thoughtful about can we even reach them with our spot beams before we change the law to say you have the right and then they can't get them.

So we'd like to participate in a fix. We think it definitely is not the intent of the law and the use of the DMA mapping. It's a well-principled concept but it's got some flaws and that's one of them.

Senator PRYOR. And just to follow up on that. You mentioned this Nielsen map, is that still a map that everybody else uses today or is that a map that satellite folks——

Mr. PALKOVIC. It is the same. I believe it's amended from time-to-time and we have to change our database on ZIP codes, occasionally. It's not often and they're not big changes but it does get tweaked from time to time but it's essentially the same maps. It's a 50-year-old map.

Senator PRYOR. Senator Smith, I'd like to give you a chance to respond.

Senator SMITH. Mr. Chairman, Thomas Jefferson once wisely suggested that new state boundaries be drawn on irrigation districts. I would suggest to you that's about how Nielsen DMAs are formulated.

And the issue you raise is one that bedeviled me every year I served in the Senate. And to Direct's credit, they're bringing stuff into Little Rock, Arkansas to cable's credit. They worked very well with us. We are entirely anxious to help but we're not the whole answer. I'm just telling you broadcasters will help you fix this and the technology exists.

For example, I have cable in Pendleton, Oregon that lets me get Oregon content but my satellite subscription from Direct does not. And I heard in more town halls, I like the Ducks and the Beavers, I hate the Huskies and the Cougars and I want Oregon content. And they can do two signals. The technology exists right now.

We're ready and we'll help you solve it when it comes up in your particular case but we can't do it alone.

Senator PRYOR. All right.

Let me ask Mr. Lake a follow-up on that, as well. I know that the FCC at one point said, you know, 614(h) might be a useful model. Can you explain that?

Mr. LAKE. Yes.

We do have authority on the cable side to do what's called a "market modification," which would address the problem that's been described by adding a station to the service area for purposes of carriage.

We don't have that authority with respect to satellite. I can't address the technological issues. It is a different technology and I don't know how difficult it would be to implement that. But, we lack the authority to make those modifications for satellite that we have for cable.

Senator PRYOR. OK.

Senator Blunt.

Senator BLUNT. Thank you, Chairman. Thank you for giving me a chance to ask a couple more questions

Mr. Palkovic, it's come to my attention that for over a year there has been an ongoing carriage dispute between your company and an independent network, The Inspiration Network. Inspiration provides family-friendly programming. There's a high demand for that kind of programming in Missouri and across the country.

I clearly think you have the right to negotiate this however you want to. At the same time, I'm told that your company wants to charge Inspiration to carry their programming while, at the same time, it's paying to carry programming from other networks that have a fraction of the viewership of Inspiration Network. Do you have a comment on that?

Mr. PALKOVIC. Well, let me respond this way. As you can imagine, all of these programming relationships are confidential; we're not allowed to disclose terms and conditions. We're bound by the agreement. We had a relationship with Inspiration Network that was perfectly fine. They wanted to extend it on significantly more favorable terms than they had, then, under. Now we pay some, some people pay us and some people are neutral. It just depends on the evaluation of the quality of the channel. It's their evaluation as well as ours.

They elected to take their channel down from DIRECTV because they didn't want to pay even close to similar terms for their carriage. So the economic relationship, as it was, was fine. They wanted to change it. We're willing to negotiate with them in good faith and, to be honest, we're still negotiating with them. There's still ongoing discussions with them. Hopefully, something gets worked out.

But, that's the way these things happens, is one party or the other gets too far apart on evaluation and somebody makes a decision to drop the channel. In this case, it happened to be their decision.

As far as evaluating one channel versus another, that's something we do every day. That's the business we're in. We have to make a judgment call on who gets paid, who pays us, and who's in between, and how much. So it's not going to shock you that normally the programmer's opinion of the value that they bring to the table is usually greater than what the distributer thinks it is. And that's where the negotiation starts.

Senator BLUNT. I assume you know how to monitor that, don't you? Don't you know how many people watch these programs?

Mr. PALKOVIC. There's some capability but not as much as you would think.

Senator BLUNT. Apparently not.

Mr. PALKOVIC. Well, look, there are privacy laws and stuff that we're not going to violate by, you know, being accused of Big Brother tactics and things. There's ways to monitor viewership of channels by third parties as opposed to us monitoring individual viewership data. There's rules around that we have to be careful with.

Mr. WOOD. Senator, I would just note that—I'm sorry. I would note that Parent's Television Council is a group that we worked with to advocate for à la carte solutions and this issue of empowering consumers and cable and satellite customers to make those choices for themselves. It's not a partisan issue. And that's a place where we have definitely worked with groups across the political spectrum to, again, give people the choice of which channels they want to buy and give them more view into how much they're paying for them.

Senator BLUNT. Right.

I do believe that Inspiration Network would say that they have significantly changed their programming from when they first made an agreement with DIRECTV and offer a different value and a lot more programming that's not as much religious broadcasting in nature as it is family friendly in nature. And I suppose that I'd have to think about whether or not all these relationships are totally private and don't relate to each other.

But, if you're paying somebody like, say, Al Jazeera to put their news on DirecTV and you're charging somebody like The Inspiration Network that has more viewers, I have a hard time figuring out the economics of that and I'm interested in it. And maybe we can talk about it some more.

Mr. Wood, earlier, the Chairman asked, Chairman Pryor asked a question. I thought you wanted to respond either to Mr. Rogers or to that overall question of the CableCARD. Did you have something you wanted to say there?

Mr. WOOD. Sure. Thank you, Senator.

I would just say, just to finish that thought on the CableCARD discussion, the integration ban is not about CableCARD. So we shouldn't conflate the two. It's about, as Mr. Rogers has explained, ensuring that we have a common standard. So no one, including consumer groups like ours, is advocating for perpetual continuation of CableCARD but simply to have a market in these devices where people can make those choices for themselves and can go buy one at retail or get it from their satellite or cable provider.

Senator BLUNT. And, Mr. Powell, the arena we're in now, where there are so many other ways to get content but a lot of that content comes through the equipment that you put in somebody's house, how are you dealing with that? In the past, you might have been the sole provider, but now the environment for broadband and pay-TV services is so much more competitive. Do you want to talk just a little bit about that?

I'm interested in how we, in this rapidly changing environment, how we adjust whether there's any realistic possibility that Congress could possibly keep up with these changes or not. But I'm interested in how you're adjusting to all these new competitors who are out there that probably use your streaming equipment to get in a house.

Mr. POWELL. Thank you, Senator, for the question. I'll try to be succinct.

I think cable companies are increasingly becoming agnostic about the method and way or device that consumers get access to the services and content that we provide because we're being driven by customer preferences in the market. A day doesn't go buy where somebody talks about a millennial who doesn't want to subscribe to cable. A day doesn't go by where I don't hear a story of someone sitting on a couch with their 4-year-old watching television on an iPad. You know, a day doesn't go by without reading some tech-net story about a new device, whether Roku, or Apple TV, or a streaming service like Netflix, or VUDU, on how that's changing the video marketplace.

If cable companies don't evolve with that and make sure they chase the consumer where they want to be and allow consumers to use the equipment and devices that they prefer, we're going to be in a tough spot. And I think the most enlightened companies in the industry are working very, very hard to empower any device that might be the preference of the consumer to receive the service and content we provide.

In fact, some companies who are competitors are doing it so well they're not just offering alternative equipment; they're offering, in essence, alternative services that can serve as a complement and more often a substitute to the services we provide. So, we do lose cord-cutting customers to alternate device systems including alternate content sources that they're able to secure in the marketplace. And I think that's going to continue to be a hot competitive space that changes our perspective on that.

Senator BLUNT. Mr. Chairman——

Mr. ROGERS. Just to respond to that, we're well aware of some cable operators trying to allow their service in some limited respect to be made available through other devices. But, those that are out there doing it allow a subset of their content to be received on other devices. You don't to have the ability to record on those other devices. You don't have the ability to have a different user interface that you may like better than the cable operator provides as a way to frame how you're accessing that cable-operator provided content. You don't have the ability to integrate Internet content into that user experience provided by the cable operator.

It's a highly limited fashion by which some of these multi-device experiments have been put forward. That shouldn't be confused at all with allowing consumers to come with their own retail set-top box that allows for the core of their television experience where they spend the vast majority of their time watching broadcast and cable channels and have a true alternative for that. That's what Mr. Markey's amendment, back in 1996, was intended to provide a regime for and that's really the guts of what the CableCARD or common reliance or integration ban is all about.

Senator BLUNT. Does anybody else have anything to say on this topic?

Thank you, Mr. Chairman.

Senator PRYOR. Thank you.

We do want to allow Senator Markey to ask other questions.

Now, Mr. Rogers, I understand you may have a flight that you're trying to get to and if you——

Mr. ROGERS. I think that's a lost cause, but thank you, Senator. [Laughter.]

Senator PRYOR. We got a late start, you know that. But anyway, if you wanted to, we would certainly excuse you to try to do that. But we'd love for you to stay if you can, but we understand.

Senator Markey.

Senator MARKEY. Thank you, Mr. Chairman.

And, again, I don't want to take any more time than we already have and we thank all of you for your patience.

You know, when the Soviet Union was falling, Gorbachev called it "perestroika," we had a restructure. And they were destroying the old but they hadn't invented the new yet. So with the CableCARD, that's what we're talking about. We're talking about well, we'll all live with the CableCARD going. We can save some energy, we can have a new era, but we have to invent the new, too. We have to have a new standard.

So, what would you recommend, Mr. Wood, for the process that we would go through if we were going to eliminate the CableCARD so that we could have a new standard that all of the participants then said, "That's fine. We can live with that new era." Who goes into that room? What does the FCC, I guess, do to make sure that all of the participants are in that room, and that a new standard comes out that reflects the new technology, and we can kiss the CableCARD goodbye, but have the protections, the historical protections, still in place?

Mr. WOOD. Thank you, Senator.

Hopefully, not just the companies in play but hopefully some voices of consumer advocates as well. But I think we do have these solutions and I'm sure Mr. Rogers and Chairman Powell could talk about them as well. You've heard about in this hearing downloadable security solutions that have been developed and just haven't really gotten over the finish line because of continued doubt about things like the integration ban, different status of life for different cable companies with where they are in their digital conversion.

And I think we need to, first and foremost, maintain the principles that we have of ensuring common reliance and not pulling the rug out before we have those in place because I think the market will get there if the principles remain intact.

Senator MARKEY. Mr. Lake, could the Federal Communications Commission put together a process like that; that had all parties at the table that do this?

Mr. LAKE. We certainly have a rule and we'll do what we can to encourage the development of a new standard. We certainly see that is what is needed.

It's very difficult for the agency to impose a technology on the industry or the public interest groups. CableCARD was brought to us as a proposal. We would very much hope that we could have a new proposal brought to us, whether it's downloadable security or something equivalent. And we'll consider what we can do to try to catalyze that effort.

Senator MARKEY. All right. Thank you.

Mr. Chairman, thank you.

Senator PRYOR. Well, with that I just want to thank all of our witnesses for coming and all the time you put into this. And we really appreciate everything that you've done for the Subcommittee and appreciate all the members.

What we're going to do is we will leave the record open for 2 weeks to allow members to submit questions for the record.

We may be in touch with some of you all to answer those.

And again, we want to thank everyone for their participation and preparation. Thank all the Subcommittee members.

And, with that, we will adjourn.

Thank you.

[Whereupon, at 5:23 p.m., the hearing was adjourned.]

APPENDIX

RESPONSE TO WRITTEN QUESTION SUBMITTED BY HON. CLAIRE MCCASKILL TO
HON. GORDON SMITH

Question. Customers have a right to expect to get what they signed up for. So when a carriage dispute between a content provider and programmer results in a channel being dropped, it makes sense to me that customers should be permitted to change providers without paying an early termination fee or other penalty. Do you agree?

Answer. Cable and satellite TV customers should have flexibility in switching providers in those rare instances in which negotiations result in specific channels being dropped from programming packages that they have paid for. By their very nature, pay-TV early termination fees, which range in the industry from $240 to $480 [1], are designed to lock in customers to multi-year contracts and prevent switching to a competitor if they have legitimate concerns with the current service provider. We think this is punitive in nature and serves to lessen competition in the pay-TV industry, ultimately harming consumer choice.

We also favor refunds on pay-TV customers' monthly bills in those situations in which a TV channel is removed for an extended period of time by the cable or satellite TV provider and is not accessible to customers on that platform. We are pleased to see that some pay-TV service providers have begun to offer these refunds to customers and we believe this should become the industry norm in today's video marketplace.

RESPONSE TO WRITTEN QUESTION SUBMITTED BY HON. JOHN WALSH TO
HON. GORDON SMITH

Question. For determining eligibility for distant signals, we rely on an outdoor 20–30 foot antenna standard. It has been suggested by some that we should update that standard. As we consider reauthorizing STELA, would you recommend revisiting this issue? What impact would amending this standard have on consumers?

Answer. No, this issue should not be revisited. Congress should resist this effort by DISH and DIRECTV to expand the scope of this license by having more subscribers receiving their network programming from distant out-of-market stations and fewer subscribers viewing this programming on their local stations. Following the 2010 reauthorization, the FCC carefully considered and rejected an indoor antenna standard for the eligibility to receive distant signals for a number of reasons. [2] First, Congress specified a specific signal strength standard to determine eligibility to receive distant signals. Second, there is no way to predict signal strength using an indoor antenna as interference factors include performance characteristics of the antenna, location of antenna (window vs. basement), proximity to electronic equipment, height, and direction of antenna. Hence, the FCC concluded that: "It would be difficult, if not impossible to obtain accurate & reliable predictors of digital television signal strengths indoors" [3] Third, use of an indoor antenna standard would allow "gaming" of the system to receive distant signals by claiming use of an indoor antenna when, in fact, an outdoor antenna can or is actually being used. The FCC found: "this would remove large numbers of viewers from local stations' potential audience. . .The Commission does not believe that Congress envisioned or contemplated such as increase in the numbers of satellite subscribers eligible for deliv-

---

[1] *See* the Dish Network's Legal Terms of its Service Commitment Agreement, early termination fees, online: *http://www.dish.com/legal/offers/*

See Mediacom Cable's Legal Terms of its Service Commitment Agreement, early termination fees, online: *https://mediacomcable.com/site/legal.html?page=legal_promotional_text.html*

[2] See, Satellite Television Extension and Localism Act of 2010 and Satellite Home Viewer Extension and Reauthorization Act of 2004, ET Docket No. 10–152, 75 FR 80354 (Dec. 22, 2010) Paras 15–18

[3] *Id.*

ery of distant network signals."[4] Fourth, DISH Network provides local-into-local service in all 210 DMAs, thereby substantially reducing the need to rely on the distant signal license, and revealing that changes to the antenna standard are being sought as an end-run around the retransmission consent process. Rather than growing the number of households that receive "local" broadcast programming from New York and Los Angeles, we would encourage you to work with DIRECTV on offering local service in Glendive and Helena, markets currently being neglected by the second largest pay-TV provider in the country. DIRECTV's failure to serve these and similar markets with local broadcast signals is a consumer disservice and public safety hazard to rural America.

———

RESPONSE TO WRITTEN QUESTION SUBMITTED BY HON. DAN COATS TO
WILLIAM T. LAKE

Question. My understanding is that the standard for measuring whether a home can get a broadcast over-the-air signal involves using a 30-foot antenna on their roof. I travel all over Indiana on a regular basis, and I cannot remember the last time I saw a 30-foot antenna on a home. In fact, I am not even sure where one would purchase a 30-foot antenna. Where did this standard come from, and should it be changed to reflect the smaller, more compact indoor antennas that consumers can purchase at any store?

Answer. In 1998, the Commission developed a model for predicting when a household is "unserved" and thus eligible to receive distant signals via satellite. That model was based on the National Telecommunications and Information Administration's "Individual Location Longley Rice" (ILLR) radio signal propagation methodology, which is used to predict the coverage of television signals by industry and government alike. In the Satellite Home Viewer Improvement Act of 1999 (SHVIA), Congress endorsed the Commission's ILLR predictive model to be used as the means of predicting whether households were served by an over-the-air broadcast signal for purposes of eligibility to receive satellite-delivered distant signals. In addition to the predictive model, SHVIA created a testing regime to measure signals as received by a household. Both the predictive model and the testing regime consider the signal based on its availability for reception at the location of the household; that is, as available 20 or 30 feet above the ground (20 feet is used for one story homes, 30 feet for homes two or more stories). The Commission's rules have traditionally used an outdoor antenna mounted at 30 feet (a "rooftop" antenna) as the standard for TV reception in defining the service areas of broadcast television stations.

Initially, the rules applied only to analog signals, but the Commission reviewed and updated its rules to account for the digital television transition in compliance with Satellite Home Viewer Extension and Reauthorization Act (SHVERA) in 2004. The ILLR predictive model was revised to measure the presence and strength of a digital television signal at 30 feet from the ground (or 20 feet if the home in question is one story). This model provides accurate, reliable and repeatable results.

In 2010, the Satellite Television Extension and Localism Act (STELA) removed the statutory limitation to "outdoor" antennas in the distant signal statutory license. In compliance with STELA, the Commission again considered the digital signal strength standard to determine if reliance on an indoor measurement would provide more reliable results in predicting whether a household is served or unserved. The Commission affirmed the prior determinations that creation of an indoor TV signal measurement procedure would be difficult due to the wide variation in the construction of homes, possible placement of the antenna within the home, and the performance and quality of indoor antennas. Further, the Commission noted that STELA specified the use of the digital television signal strength standard in Section 73.622(e)(1) of the Commission's rules as the threshold to determine whether households are served or unserved. This rule is premised on the use of an outdoor antenna, and the Commission concluded that it was appropriate to retain the same requirements for the signal strength measurement standards. At the time, proponents of relying on indoor antennas as the basis for the standard did not provide the Commission with a reliable indoor testing method, and we believe that nothing has changed siilce that time to warrant a re-examination of this issue.

———

[4] *Id.*

RESPONSE TO WRITTEN QUESTION SUBMITTED BY HON. CLAIRE MCCASKILL TO MICHAEL W. PALKOVIC

Question. Customers have a right to expect to get what they signed up for. So when a carriage dispute between a content provider and programmer results in a channel being dropped, it makes sense to me that customers should be permitted to change providers without paying an early termination fee or other penalty. Do you agree?

Answer. DIRECTV does not *require* customers to pay an early termination fee if they change providers early. Rather, customers can *choose* to enter into a programming agreement (which contains such fees) in exchange for steep discounts on DIRECTV equipment and programming approaching $800 in total. For example, without these discounts/credits, an average customer would pay $397 (1 HD DVR @ $199 + 2 HD clients @ $198) for equipment, and would pay $384 more in programming costs based on our CHOICE package. Customers can always pay full price without entering a programming agreement, in which case they are free to leave any time. But most prefer to spread those additional costs over the life of a programming agreement.

Our programming contracts are also fair in other respects. They clearly state in plain English that programming and channel lineups are subject to change and that such changes do not permit either party to terminate the agreement. We carry multiple channels in several programming genres. For example, we carry 18 independent networks carrying faith based programming: BYU TV, CTN, Church Channel, Daystar, EWTN, INCTV, GOD TV, GEB America, Hope, Jewish Life Television, NRB, Son Life, TCT Network, The Word Network, TBN, TBN Enlace USA, Up, and World Harvest Television. And we "pro-rate" early termination fees based on how long the subscriber has left on her agreement.

We would like to raise one last point. We do not "drop" broadcasters. Broadcasters force us to drop their signals by withholding "consent" if we do not agree to massive price increases. We absolutely agree that our subscribers have a right to expect the programming they signed up for. This is exactly why Congress should consider ways to reduce or (better yet) eliminate blackouts.

————

RESPONSE TO WRITTEN QUESTION SUBMITTED BY HON. JOHN WALSH TO MICHAEL W. PALKOVIC

Question. My constituents have written me to ask for access to in-state Montana local broadcasters. In eight Montana counties, "local" broadcast stations come from outside Montana. One county is even forced to watch "local" stations from Washington state, two states away. This leaves Montanans in these counties without the opportunity to watch local news and weather or key coverage like the annual "Cat-Griz" football game between Montana State University and the University of Montana. Is there an appropriate way to remedy this situation as we renew STELA?

Answer. We, too, are concerned about subscribers in what have become known as "orphan counties." Many of these subscribers want "local" stations from their own states. They want not only in-state news, but also in-state sports and entertainment programming. We succeed in the marketplace by giving our subscribers what they want. But right now, we can't, in part because the law prevents us from doing so, and we thus support efforts to change the law.

You should, however, be aware of three other factors relevant to this discussion. First, we carry local stations on "spot beams" that cover limited geographic areas. We thus are not technically capable of carrying in-state stations to all orphan counties. Second, most subscribers—even those that want in-state stations—do not want to lose the stations they already have. Third, the retransmission consent fees charged by local stations have gone through the roof. A "solution" that requires all subscribers in orphan counties to pay double (or more) their local stations is no solution at all. We thus support targeted legislation that would give us the option of adding in-state stations in orphan counties where we can. Such legislation would also give orphan county subscribers the choice of taking such in-state stations, and would limit the amount subscribers would have to pay for these new stations—while still fairly compensating broadcasters and copyright holders.

RESPONSE TO WRITTEN QUESTION SUBMITTED BY HON. KELLY AYOTTE TO
MICHAEL W. PALKOVIC

Question. As we have heard today, the video market is extremely competitive and vibrant. In fact, with 33 million customers in the United States, Netflix has more subscribers than any other single multichannel video provider. Do your industry is competing on a level playing field? Are there any regulations that put you at a competitive advantage or disadvantage?

Answer. As we discussed in the Joint Written Response of DIRECTV and DISH, submitted to the Committee on March 17, 2014 ("Joint Response"), a panoply of regulations give broadcasters preferential treatment. (We provided a list of these regulations as Exhibit A to the Joint Response). These regulations, individually and collectively, result in a "competitive disadvantage" for DIRECTV. More importantly, they result in increased blackouts and higher prices for DIRECTV's subscribers.

In addition, online-based "over the top" ("OTT") providers generally are not subject to significant FCC regulation. This means both that they are free from the burdens such regulation place on more traditional MVPDs and that they often cannot avail themselves of the protections contained in such regulation. Generally speaking, DIRECTV has supported equal treatment for providers offering similar services, regardless of the platform used.

———

RESPONSE TO WRITTEN QUESTION SUBMITTED BY HON. DAN COATS TO
MICHAEL W. PALKOVIC

Question. My understanding is that the standard for measuring whether a home can get a broadcast over-the-air signal involves using a 30-foot antenna on their roof. I travel all over Indiana on a regular basis, and I cannot remember the last time I saw a 30-foot antenna on a home. In fact, I am not even sure where one would purchase a 30-foot antenna. Where did this standard come from, and should it be changed to reflect the smaller, more compact indoor antennas that consumers can purchase at any store?

Answer. As discussed in more detail in Question I(4) of our Joint Response, the law has for years specified that households would be considered "served" (and thus ineligible for distant signals) if tested or predicted to receive signals of a specified strength using a "conventional, stationary, outdoor rooftop receiving antenna." This standard was developed in the early days of broadcasting, and was originally used to help set generalized "service contours" for analog broadcasters so that they did not interfere with one another. This never really had anything to do with the equipment that people actually used back then—and certainly has no relationship to the equipment they use today.

Moreover, as your question suggests, this standard is a terrible way to measure eligibility for distant signals. Subscribers should be able to receive *distant* signals if they cannot receive a viewable *local* signal over the air. But assuming that every subscriber has a perfectly calibrated rooftop antenna—when almost nobody has such equipment—means that many people who should be eligible for distant signals are not.

Not only *should* the standard be changed to reflect antennas used today, but Congress *already made* such a change. Five years ago, Congress removed the words "conventional, stationary, outdoor rooftop receiving" before the word "antenna." The plain intent was to (as you put it) "reflect the smaller, more compact indoor antennas that consumers can purchase at any store." Unfortunately, however, the FCC failed to implement this change. We urge Congress to take more definitive action to help the FCC rectify its error.

———

RESPONSE TO WRITTEN QUESTION SUBMITTED BY HON. TIM SCOTT TO
MICHAEL W. PALKOVIC

Question. With the widespread adoption of subscription-based video platforms by consumers, we are seeing the development of a diverse range of content by independent television networks, sometimes tailored to the interests of previously underserved consumers. But it can often be a substantial challenge for these independent networks to gain carriage on subscription-based platforms, and it seems the process can be rather opaque from their perspective. Can you give us some insight into the factors DirectTV uses in making carriage decisions?

Answer. We attempt to make carriage decisions based on what our subscribers want to watch. We are, however, limited in several respects, including the following:

- Our satellite system has limited capacity—especially with respect to local and regional programming.
- We are subject to series of regulatory carriage requirements that apply to us, including "carry-one, carry-all" for local broadcast channels and a four percent set-aside for "qualified programmers for noncommercial programming of an educational or informational nature."
- We are often required by large programming conglomerates to carry unpopular networks as the price of carrying popular ones.

Each of these three limitations makes it more difficult for us to carry independent channels that we might otherwise wish to carry.

Unlike some of our larger competitors, DIRECTV is largely unaffiliated with programmers. (We own a minority interest in Game Show Network and own three regional sports networks.) Many people worry that so-called "vertically integrated" cable operators make programming decisions to benefit their programming affiliates. We believe that such worries do not apply to us.

———

RESPONSE TO WRITTEN QUESTIONS SUBMITTED BY HON. CLAIRE McCASKILL TO HON. MICHAEL K. POWELL

Question 1. Consumer Reports recently published a survey of more than 80,000 cable subscribers that found an astonishing 92 percent of respondents who called to negotiate with their cable company were able to get a better deal. Consumers shouldn't have to call their provider every six months in order to get a fair shake. I would think businesses would want to do everything they can to keep customers from dropping their service or changing providers but instead it often takes the threat of doing just that to get the best deal available. Being charged a premium for HD channels even after HD channels are standard, being charged a premium for higher Internet speeds once the higher speed is the base speed, having "promotions" end that would likely be renewed if a customer picked up the phone—these are among the examples I've heard from constituents about and even experienced myself. How does this pricing model best serve your customers? Do you have statistics or an estimate on what percentage of cable customers contact customer service on an annual basis to renegotiate their rate?

Answer. Cable operators today are constantly innovating to offer new options and bundles of services tailored to fit the full spectrum of consumer preference. Customers can select packages that include a variety of tiered options for basic through premium cable; can add on DVR or on-demand capabilities; and can opt to receive bundles of services, including phone and Internet, all at varying service and price levels. Our companies make full information about their range of service and pricing offerings readily available to their subscribers, including by describing them online and through mailed inserts and other means of direct communication, so that customers can compare and contrast multiple options, and choose the best service at the best price for them. Cable believes that giving consumers the information they need to make informed choices and an enhanced ability to tailor and control what they receive best serves our customers. Our customers take full advantage of the information they receive, and review their service offerings not just annually, but frequently, adjusting their service as necessary to benefit from the latest offerings, either by contacting customer service, or by accessing their account and making changes online.

Question 2. I have a TiVo. I like my TiVo. I assure you I do not want to put TiVO out of business. NCTA has proposed eliminating the so-called set-top box "integration ban" that requires a CableCard be installed in every leased set-top box even though the leased box could be built without a card. The intent was good but as a practical matter technology has moved past the CableCard, and eliminating this technology mandate could reduce the cost of the boxes as well as reduce their energy consumption—a win-win, as long as we can ensure cable providers are still supporting and not discriminating against commercial set-top boxes like Tivo. If Congress does what you are advocating and directs the FCC to eliminate the "integration ban," why would the industry still support CableCards?

Question 2a. It is my understanding that the FCC would still have authority under Section 629 of the Communications Act to ensure commercial availability of set-top boxes; in fact isn't there a separate rule today that cable would still have to comply with? And if you did not comply, wouldn't the FCC be empowered to take action, including fine a company if it failed to comply?

Answer. Even if the integration ban is repealed, cable operators will have strong marketplace incentives to support CableCARDs. First, over 47 million legacy

CableCARD-enabled leased set-top boxes are deployed today and are used by cable operators to deliver service. Second, consumers with third party devices are still cable customers and cable operators are strongly motivated to attract and retain these customers in a highly competitive market. No rule ordered cable to serve tablets, smartphones, Xbox, PCs, Macs, or SmartTVs, but that market imperative led cable to support those devices using new technologies that they do not use in their own leased set-top boxes.

We have a good test case proving that market imperative. Cablevision has used downloadable security rather than CableCARDs in its leased set-top boxes since 2011, but it has continued to provide CableCARDs to customers for use in retail devices and to support TiVo.

The proposed repeal of the integration ban is narrow: it only repeals the integration ban, an FCC rule which is not part of the statute, and preserves all other FCC authority. As a regulatory backstop, the FCC can continue to enforce a different rule—unaffected by repeal of the integration ban—that requires cable operators to offer a "separable security" solution for retail devices which for most operators means CableCARDs. The FCC monitors the market by requiring CableCARD inventory, deployment, price and trouble reports every 90 days from the five largest cable operators; it has existing complaint procedures to consider any disputes over whether CableCARDs are performing; and it may issue enforcement orders which can include fines and forfeitures for non-compliance.

Question 3. Customers have a right to expect to get what they signed up for. So when a carriage dispute between a content provider and programmer results in a channel being dropped, it makes sense to me that customers should be permitted to change providers without paying an early termination fee or other penalty. Do you agree?

Answer. The cable industry takes seriously our obligation to provide clear and accurate information about the variety of service plans that we offer to meet consumers' needs.

Our companies typically offer all of their services on a month to month basis. But in addition, they sometimes try to meet their consumers' needs through promotional offers, where consumers can benefit from lower prices in exchange for committing to a defined contract term (for example, a year). While these promotions are popular among many customers, customers who prefer a month-to-month plan generally always have that alternative.

In the rare instance in which a customer that has elected to be part of a promotional contract elects to switch before the term has ended, the cable operator may seek to recoup some the promotional benefit extended under the original contract term. Typically, these ETFs or "breakup fees" are prorated based on the remaining time left in the contract term. Our practices are consistent regardless of a customer's reason for ending the contract term early. While we never want customers to switch, our aim is to treat all customers fairly, and consistent with the terms of their service arrangement.

———

RESPONSE TO WRITTEN QUESTION SUBMITTED BY HON. KELLY AYOTTE TO HON. MICHAEL K. POWELL

Question. One of the provisions in STELA requires broadcasters and pay-tv providers to negotiate "in good faith". When I look at the spiraling upward trend of blackouts, having gone from 12 blackouts in 2010 to 127 blackouts in 2013, it is hard to believe this provision is working as intended. Can you talk about your perspective or definition of what "in good faith" means?

Answer. NCTA supports the reauthorization of the mutual "in good faith" retransmission consent provisions in Section 325 of the Communications Act. Broadcast programming remains an important part of the cable service offering, and ensuring that negotiations for the carriage of broadcast programming on cable are conducted honestly, in a good faith attempt to reach a mutually beneficial carriage agreement without demanding unreasonable terms and conditions or taking unreasonable postures, is an important part of protecting consumers.

By a 5–0 vote, the FCC recently made joint retransmission consent negotiations among the top four stations in a local Designated Market Area a *per se* violation of a broadcaster's obligation to negotiate in good faith when the broadcasters are not commonly owned. Through statute, Congress should complement and extend the FCC's regulatory action.

RESPONSE TO WRITTEN QUESTIONS SUBMITTED BY HON. DEAN HELLER TO
HON. MICHAEL K. POWELL

Question 1. Should we make any of these changes in STELA?

Answer. Yes, STELA is an appropriate legislative vehicle to address a number of narrow, targeted video reforms, including prohibiting non-commonly owned broadcasters from coordinating their retransmission consent negotiations. This ban could be effected by modifying Section 325 of the Communications Act to prohibit these activities, or by clarifying explicitly that such coordination would violate a broadcaster's obligation to negotiate in good faith.

NCTA also supports two other reforms, repeal of the FCC's technology mandate known as the "integration ban" and elimination of retransmission consent stations from the basic "must buy" tier. These reforms would directly benefit consumers, prune away outdated legal requirements, and promote a more level playing field among multichannel video programming distributors (MVPDs).

The FCC's "integration ban" mandate forces consumers to bear needless costs, increases energy use, and precludes cable operators, and *only* cable operators, from leasing set-top boxes with less expensive and more energy-efficient decryption technologies. Unevenly applied, three of the five largest MVPDs do not comply with this tech mandate.

In carrying out Congress's directive in Section 629 of the Communications Act that the FCC adopt rules to promote a *retail* market for set-top boxes and other navigation devices, the FCC did two things. First, because different cable operators used different scrambling technologies, the FCC required cable operators to develop a separate security device to unscramble cable signals—now known as the CableCARD—for use in set-top boxes and other navigation devices that could be sold at retail and used on any cable system. If a customer moved, he could return the CableCARD to his former cable provider, and get a new CableCARD from his new cable provider. But the FCC took a second and unnecessary step of mandating that a cable operator's leased set-top boxes be redesigned to also include CableCARDs. When used in leased set-top boxes that are owned by and returned to the cable operator, CableCARDs do nothing that hadn't been done previously by leased boxes with traditional "integrated" security while wasting hundreds of millions of kilowatt hours in energy per year and forcing customers who lease set-top boxes to pay over $1 billion in added set-top box costs for portability they do not want or need in a leased box. Today there are more than 47 million CableCard devices deployed in leased set-top boxes, but only 616,000 CableCards have been requested for third-party retail devices.

Repeal of this technology mandate would eliminate the inequities forced upon cable subscribers, who choose to lease set-top boxes, while not affecting the retail market. If the integration ban is repealed, operators will have strong marketplace incentives to support CableCARDs given the over 47 million CableCARD-enabled leased set-top boxes they use to serve their customers today, and the fact that cable operators are strongly motivated to attract and retain customers with retail devices in a highly competitive market, including cable customers who use CableCARD-enabled devices like TiVos. And, as a regulatory backstop, the FCC can enforce a different rule—which would be unaffected by repeal of the integration ban—that requires cable operators to offer a "separate security" solution (*e.g.,* the CableCARD) to manufacturers of retail devices.

In addition, NCTA supports repeal of the "must buy" requirement. The Communications Act mandates that cable operators, and *only* cable operators, include *all* broadcasters on a basic tier, which *all* cable subscribers "must buy" before they can purchase any other cable programming. To give consumers and operators more flexibility, the "must buy" tier should be limited to must carry stations and certain other channels mandated by local franchises.

Broadcast stations freely electing retransmission consent should not have a government-mandated right to be included in the "must buy" basic tier. Retransmission stations could continue to negotiate placement, but would no longer enjoy the unwarranted benefit of a government-created mandate that narrows consumer choice for cable subscribers in contrast to other MVPD subscribers.

Question 2. At the very least shouldn't the laws reflect parity between cable and satellite providers?

Answer. Yes, NCTA has long advocated that laws can and should be more technology-neutral and that functionally equivalent services should be treated similarly. As noted above, cable operators remain subject to a number of statutory requirements that DBS providers are not, even though—from the consumer's perspective—they provide the same type of service and the DBS providers are the second and third largest MVPDs. Congress should examine the Communications Act broadly, to ensure that the law does not confer any regulatory advantage or disadvantage based on the use of any particular technology.

———

RESPONSE TO WRITTEN QUESTIONS SUBMITTED BY HON. CLAIRE MCCASKILL TO THOMAS S. ROGERS

Question 1. I have a TiVo. I like my TiVo. I assure you I do not want to put TiVo out of business. NCTA has proposed eliminating the so-called set-top box "integration ban" that requires a CableCard be installed in every leased set-top box even though the leased box could be built without a card. The intent was good but as a practical matter technology has moved past the CableCard, and eliminating this technology mandate could reduce the cost of the boxes as well as reduce their energy consumption—a win-win, as long as we can ensure cable providers are still supporting and not discriminating against commercial set-top boxes like Tivo. Isn't the CableCard outdated technology?

Answer. TiVo agrees that CableCARD *is* becoming an outdated technology but it is still the only industry-wide standard that will support retail boxes. The problem is that while the cable industry wants to move to a more modern security technology for its own leased boxes, it has *not* proposed a modern successor security technology for use by retail boxes. The issue is not about a ban on "integrating" security into boxes; the real issue is common reliance by operator boxes and retail boxes on the *same* security technology. Reliance on the same security technology is how we assure that cable providers do not discriminate against retail boxes.

NCTA wants to allow cable operators to use new and *different* security solutions for their own leased boxes, while claiming that operators will continue to support the use of old CableCARD technology in retail boxes. The notion of requiring retail devices to rely on different security than operator boxes is bad enough yet, at the FCC, the NCTA is arguing that *the FCC's CableCARD rules are no longer in effect and cable operators have no obligation to supply CableCARDs to retail devices.*[1]

In the absence of any FCC requirement for operators to supply CableCARDs to retail devices, the integration ban is the only thing that practically assures that CableCARDs will be supplied by operators simply because if cable operators have to use CableCARDs in their own devices, then cable operators will supply CableCARDs to retail devices. Conversely, if operators don't have to use CableCARDs in their own devices and they stop buying CableCARDs, then basic economics dictate that the CableCARD manufacturers, Motorola/Arris and Cisco, will stop making CableCARDs (or at best dramatically increase pricing) because demand will drop significantly since only competitive boxes will be using CableCARDs, there is no requirement for Motorola/Arris and Cisco to continue to manufacture them, and Motorola/Arris and Cisco do not want retail competition.

For retail boxes to be a real alternative for consumers, they need to use the same conditional access solution as operator leased boxes use to unlock the encrypted cable programming. Allowing operator boxes to use different conditional access than retail boxes will inevitably result in retail boxes not having access to all of the cable programming. A retail box that cannot receive all of your cable programming is not a viable alternative for a consumer.

TiVo simply wants to rely on the same conditional access solution that the industry relies on for its own set top boxes. When the industry comes forward with a successor solution to access their cable signals (presumably IP-based), then we can sunset CableCARD and all move on to a better solution for everyone.

Question 1a. Why aren't the protections under Section 629 of the Communications Act enough to ensure companies like Tivo can continue to compete?

Answer. Section 629 protects competitive entry only to the extent that the FCC's implementing regulations do. NCTA insists that these regulations place cable operators under no obligation to take any further steps to accommodate competitive devices such as TiVo's.

Cable operators have already announced plans to use IP to deliver some programming to be available to subscribers who lease their proprietary boxes, but not to subscribers who own retail CableCARD boxes. Cable operators insist that they are under no obligation to make equal access to their systems available on a national basis for IP-delivered signals. Absent the so-called integration ban that has required common reliance on the same security standard by operator and retail boxes, no

---

[1] *See* Comments of National Cable & Telecommunications Association, CS Docket No. 97–80, at pp. 4–5 (Feb. 14, 2014); Opposition of Charter Communications, Inc. to Petition for Reconsideration, MB Docket No. 12–328, CSR–8470–Z, at 3 (June 3, 2013) ("CableCARD support is no longer required.")

present FCC rules would address the need for a common successor standard to be provided. This would allow cable operators to provide signals via IP to their *own* devices yet withhold the same technology from any competitive product.

It is worth noting that a consequence of the NCTA's position that the FCC's CableCARD rules are not longer in effect is that the FCC's companion rules that require operators to clearly and conspicuously disclose equipment rental fees, prevent operators from charging consumers for a set-top box when the consumer is using a retail set-top box, and prevent the levying of service charges on subscribers using retail boxes that are not levied on operator boxes and other discriminatory practices against subscribers using retail equipment are similarly no longer in effect.

FCC oversight remains as relevant today as ever because the incentives for cable operators to favor their own leased equipment and discriminate against retail products remain as strong as ever. On the whole, cable operators charge consumers an estimated $7 billion each year from set-top box leasing fees.[2] At a time when cable operators are faced with rising programming costs, equipment leasing costs are one area where operators can raise revenue to boost earnings.[3] Consumer electronics prices almost always drop over time, but monthly cable set-top rental prices are rising.[4] Competition from retail devices leads to lower prices, but this has not happened in the set-top box market because consumers have limited choices. The fact that cable operators have the incentive to deny consumer choice to maintain and increase the revenue stream associated with leasing set-top boxes demonstrates the need for Congress and the FCC to ensure competition from retail devices.

Question 2. Customers have a right to expect to get what they signed up for. So when a carriage dispute between a content provider and programmer results in a channel being dropped, it makes sense to me that customers should be permitted to change providers without paying an early termination fee or other penalty. Do you agree?

Answer. TiVo agrees that costumers have a right to change providers in order to get what they pay for. However, without equivalent access to signals across cable, satellite and telco platforms, it is difficult for consumers to switch providers, particularly if they have invested in a competitive retail device. In TiVo's case, the CableCARD interface on our products could not help an unhappy customer move to a competitive satellite or "IPTV" service because the FCC has not required that retail devices have access to the signals delivered by those operators.

With IP technology this need not be the case. A common IP-level interface for devices could work not only across all cable systems and telco systems, allowing an unhappy customer to switch providers yet still keep her competitive product and any content stored on it. Access to satellite signals could also be incorporated into such a retail device. The idea of a device that could allow a consumer to switch among MVPDs has been consistently opposed by virtually every MVPD.

RESPONSE TO WRITTEN QUESTION SUBMITTED BY HON. CLAIRE MCCASKILL TO MATTHEW F. WOOD

Question. Customers have a right to expect to get what they signed up for. So when a carriage dispute between a content provider and programmer results in a channel being dropped, it makes sense to me that customers should be permitted to change providers without paying an early termination fee or other penalty. Do you agree?

Answer. Yes, Free Press agrees that customers have a right to receive the services for which they have paid. We believe it makes sense to provide relief to multichannel video program distributor ("MVPD") subscribers who lose service due to carriage disputes, including by holding them harmless against early termination fees and penalties.

---

[2] *See Report on Cable Industry Prices,* MM Docket No. 92–266, DA 13–1319, at 12–13, ¶¶ 21–22 (rel. June 7, 2013) (finding average cost of leasing a cable set-top box to be $7.29 per month; the $7 billion figure assumes 54 million subscribers nationwide and an average of 1.5 set-top boxes per home).

[3] *See David Lazarus, TWC is Offering Customers Little in Return for Its Latest Rate Hikes,* March 17, 2014, available at *http://touch.latimes.com/#section/-1/article/p2p-79650340/*

[4] *See id;* Jessica DiNapoli, *Time Warner Cable Raises Cable, Internet Rates,* Times Herald-Record, Feb. 27, 2014, available at *http://www.recordonline.com/apps/pbcs.dll/article?AID=/20140227/BIZ/402270319;* Todd Spangler, *Verizon Raising FiOS TV DVR, Set-Top Rates,* Multichannel News, Mar. 23, 2012, available at *http://www.multichannel.com/content/verizon-raising-fios-tv-dvr-set-top-rates.*

However, as explained in our written testimony, we also support measures to prevent loss of service in the first place. For instance, a "standstill" period would ensure continued carriage when negotiations reach an impasse, so that viewers are not subjected to loss of service as a negotiating tactic. Congress should clarify the Federal Communications Commission's authority to order interim carriage during a retransmission consent dispute, to the extent that the Commission does not possess this authority already.

Some parties have suggested as remedies for these situations a requirement of refunds to MVPD subscribers after a blackout ends, in addition to the early termination fee relief described in the question. Others have suggested allowing importation of distant broadcast signals when a blackout begins. Still others argue for creating a counter-productive "parity" that would let MVPDs *delete* broadcast signals during ratings periods, so that both sides in the carriage dispute have power to take down service.

In almost every case, Free Press believes preventing the loss of service in the first place would be more beneficial for viewers than any attempt to make them whole after the fact. Beyond "standstill" carriage, for which we have consistently advocated before the Commission, we also have called for passage of bills such as the Television Consumer Freedom Act of 2013 sponsored by Senators McCain, Blumenthal and Whitehouse.

Giving MVPD subscribers not just the knowledge of what they pay for each channel, but also the ability to decide whether to buy that channel at all, would bring real market forces to bear on carriage negotiations. Without such direct measures of viewer demand, broadcasters and MVPDs will fight over the price of a channel yet simply pass along all of the cost to viewers once a deal has been struck. If viewers were instead empowered to decide which channels they buy, this would allow them to vote with their wallets when the price for a particular service is too high—all contributing to a more transparent and rational pricing structure than the forced bundling model viewers must deal with today.

○